McGraw-Hill Education

500 Review Questions for the MCAT: Behavioral Sciences

Koni S. Christensen, MS, CHES

New York Chicago San Francisco Athens London Madrid
Mexico City Milan New Delhi Singapore Sydney Toronto

1 2 3 4 5 6 7 8 9   DOC   21 20 19 18 17 16

ISBN   978-0-07-184139-9
MHID   0-07-184139-3

e-ISBN   978-0-07-183746-0
e-MHID   0-07-183746-9

MCAT is a registered trademark of the Association of American Medical Colleges, which was not involved in the production of, and does not endorse, this product.

McGraw-Hill Education products are available at special quantity discounts to use as premiums and sales promotions or for use in corporate training programs. To contact a representative, please visit the Contact Us pages at www.mhprofessional.com.

CONTENTS

Introduction   v
About the Author   vi

Chapter 1   **Biological Theories and Perspectives   1**
Questions 1–75

Chapter 2   **Nature versus Nurture: Perspectives on Individual Differences   17**
Questions 76–175

Chapter 3   **Stages of Psychosocial Development   43**
Questions 176–236

Chapter 4   **Behavioral Theories and Perspectives   59**
Questions 237–320

Chapter 5   **Cognitive Theories and Perspectives   77**
Questions 321–443

Chapter 6   **Social Theories and Perspectives   105**
Questions 444–500

Answers   121

References   169

INTRODUCTION

You've taken a big step toward MCAT success by purchasing *500 Review Questions for the MCAT: Behavioral Sciences.* We are here to help you take the next step and score high on the MCAT so you can get into the medical school of your choice.

This book will help you prepare for the biopsychosocial section of the MCAT, Psychological, Social, and Biological Foundations of Behavior. It is organized to familiarize you with the various psychological theories that have been developed to better understand human behavior and health. Its reading passages highlight how biological/physiological, social, and environmental influences work together to shape human health. As you read them, not only will you gain valuable practice for the exam, you will be able to review the theories and concepts covered by the test.

Here you will find 500 questions that cover all the most essential material. The questions will give you valuable independent practice to supplement your regular textbooks and the ground you have already covered in your classes. They will help you form a foundation for understanding biopsychosocial behavior patterns and the ways in which people are influenced by social systems. The questions after each reading passage are divided into three kinds: multiple choice, fill in the blank, and short answer. This mix of questions will help keep you engaged as you study as well as encourage you to think critically. The answers provides comprehensive explanations for more in-depth questions.

This book and the others in the 500 series were written by expert teachers who know the MCAT subject matter inside and out and can identify crucial information as well as the kinds of questions that are most likely to appear on the exam.

You might be the kind of student who needs to study extra a few weeks before the exam for a final review. Or you might be the kind of student who puts off preparing until the last minute before the exam. No matter what your preparation style, you will benefit from reviewing these 500 questions. If you practice with all the questions and answers in this book, we are certain you will build the skills and confidence needed to excel on the MCAT. Good luck!

—*The Editors of McGraw-Hill Education*

ABOUT THE AUTHOR

Koni S. Christensen MS, CHES teaches general psychology and human growth and development psychology and is the owner of a private wellness business. She has worked in behavior modification settings and has written extensively on behavioral health–related issues.

CHAPTER 1

Biological Theories and Perspectives

Nativism, Philosophical Empiricism, and Dualism

Psychology originated from early health philosophy and physiology, dating back to the dominant belief that spirits were responsible for health status by bringing good health or illness when they entered the body. The belief that health or illness was a gift or punishment from God grew from this perspective. The Greeks were the first to introduce the idea of health being holistic, of the mind and spirit, although the concepts were not well understood. Progressively the belief moved toward physiology and the effect of pathogens on the physical and emotional state of the body. Although research continues to seek to understand and provide explanations for health and illness, the emphasis on God's influence on an individual's health or wellness has never lapsed.

Hippocrates was the first to introduce health from a perspective other than superstitious beliefs, and he later became known as the "Father of Medicine." Hippocrates's early knowledge of the body, though vastly inaccurate, asserted that illness and sickness have natural causes and therefore need natural treatment. This was contrary to popular beliefs, which held that illness and disease are punishments from God and cured only by God through exorcisms or charms. Hippocrates believed that the fluids within the body—bile, phlegm, and blood—were responsible for explaining psychological characteristics of people. The four humors theory was widely accepted among ancient physicians. In addition to providing early perspectives to describing physical and psychological health, Hippocrates brought forth the first ethical guidelines for medicine, now known as "first, do no harm" and deeply embedded in current medical practice and human research as the Hippocratic oath.

The Greek philosophers Socrates, Plato, and Aristotle were among the first to begin theorizing about human behaviors. Plato theorized that life existed in somewhat of a cycle, what we might consider reincarnation. Knowledge from the previous life somehow makes it into the mind of the new life, and therefore some types of knowledge are innate. In other words, we are born with some knowledge because the life we lived before knew it, a view that has come to be known as nativism. Though a student of Plato, Aristotle built his framework around the idea of the *tabula rasa*: he held that at birth, the mind resembles a blank slate. Aristotle proposed philosophical empiricism, the theory that experiences create knowledge and learning through observation, counter to the inherited knowledge of nativism.

René Descartes, a French philosopher, was the first to define the mind-body connection. Descartes believed in dualism, the concept that the mind and body are distinct from each other but interact and influence each other. Descartes proposed that the influence was bidirectional, and the body was like a machine. His theories relied on laws of physics and chemistry and included the belief the nerves were hollow tubes through which animal spirits would flow in response to external stimulus. He asserted that the only purpose of the mind was thought (the mental element), and the body (the physical element) was responsible for generating everything else, including movement and reproduction. This perspective inspired exploration of the nervous system and helped bring awareness to how external stimulus influences the body.

Building from the doctrine of ideas proposed by Descartes and the *tabula rasa* concept of Aristotle, John Locke, an English philosopher, described attainment of knowledge as a result of sensations and reflections, or meanings given to these sensations. He proposed that reflection immediately follows sensory experiences, and there is an accumulated effect over time. In other words, we give meaning to new sensations by reflecting on earlier experiences. Locke applied this philosophy to explain variances in human perceptions. For example, tangible qualities such as weight and dimension can be consistently measured. On the other hand, complex qualities such as taste, smell, and color experiences are not consistent from one person to the next. Perception of an experience defines the experience in the present, and also works as knowledge for future experiences. Moreover, people can add bits of their own knowledge to both the tangible and complex qualities of events, making it less likely that perceptions of the same phenomena will be defined in the same way by all people, every time.

Multiple-Choice Questions

1. Psychology is defined as the scientific study of
    (A) animals and humans
    (B) emotion and behaviors
    (C) the body and brain
    (D) the mind and behavior

2. Psychology originated from

(A) physiology and philosophy
(B) health and dogma
(C) dogma and philosophy
(D) health and physiology

3. Which of the following promoted the idea that we are born with certain types of knowledge?

(A) Plato
(B) Descartes
(C) Aristotle
(D) Galen

4. Philosophical empiricism is the idea that knowledge is the result of experience and learning results from

(A) good breeding
(B) flow of phlegm
(C) observation
(D) nurture

5. Philosophical empiricism is to Aristotle as _____ is to Plato.

(A) dualism
(B) Hippocratic oath
(C) nativism
(D) evolution

6. _____ holds that we are born with some knowledge because the life we lived before knew it.

(A) Dualism
(B) Hippocratic oath
(C) Nativism
(D) Evolution

7. _____, the first ethical guidelines for medical research and practice, was brought forth by early Greek writings of Hippocrates.

(A) Dualism
(B) The Hippocratic oath
(C) Nativism
(D) Evolution

Fill-in-the-Blank Questions

8. Psychology's roots can be traced back to ancient _____.

9. What did Aristotle mean by *tabula rasa*?

10. Observable actions of human beings refers to _____, while the inner experiences of perceptions, thoughts, memories, and feelings refers to the _____.

11. John Locke proposed that knowledge is attained as a result of _____ and _____.

12. Descartes believed in _____, the concept that the mind and body are separate but interact together and influence each other.

13. Variances in reflections were explained by Locke as reflections having a/an _____over time.

14. The debate between empiricism and nativism continues today but is known as _____.

Short-Answer Questions

15. Since humans began thinking about behaviors, what question have philosophers been seeking to understand?

16. How did early philosophy influence psychology?

17. What is the primary disagreement between empiricism and nativism? Explain why this disagreement is still active today.

18. In what way did Descartes initiate the trend of the mind-body connection?

19. John Locke believed in empiricism, that no knowledge whatsoever is innate. Describe Locke's perspective on sensation and reflection experiences.

Physiology and Psychology

Philosophers played a key role in paving the way for the science of psychology, and physiologists made it possible for psychology to continue to grow and develop. Early physiologists such as Johannes Müller (1801–1858) sparked experimental research and curiosity about the nervous system's function in human behavior. Once experiments on sensory nerves became the focal point, mapping the brain soon followed. Researchers including physicians, physiologists, and biologists quickly discovered that reflexive responses could occur by stimulating particular areas of the brain. Likewise, if an area in the brain or spinal cord was damaged or destroyed, scientists were able to detect subsequent changes in responses, or in some cases, a lack of response. Within a few years, clinical brain research on humans, including autopsies and electrical stimulation, was taking place in hospital settings.

Leading the way was Franz Joseph Gall (1758–1828), a French physician interested in mental functions and the mind-brain relationship. Gall studied diseased brains of humans and animals that had died, and he made many contributions such as the discovery of white and gray matter, and the organization of nerve connections in the brain to the opposite side of the spinal cord. Gall was among the first to suggest that brains with advanced mental abilities were larger, contributing to what we accept today as atrophy in brain areas that have been damaged. Gall also made a keen assertion that different areas of the brain were responsible for particular mental activities. At the time, there was no scientific way to discover and thereby validate Gall's claim. Instead, he believed the shape of the brain could provide evidence to support this theory, which he called phrenology, and that the dents and bumps of the skull defined the shape of the brain below it. Phrenology was temporarily popular as a way to screen employees, assess intelligence in children, and identify many emotional problems in day-to-day life. However, physiologists quickly discounted the original claims with the discovery that the skull shape did not match the brain shape and that the brain maps created by Gall and other phrenologists contained many errors.

Today we know that there was some truth to Gall's idea of specific areas of the brain for particular mental activities. While phrenology failed as a scientific method, the idea of specific areas of the brain being responsible for particular behaviors grew. Researchers soon began to explore dissections in living animals to study behavior changes and continued to study human brains in deceased patients.

In the 1860s, a surgeon by the name of Paul Broca (1824–1880) made a remarkable discovery of a key area in the brain that is responsible for spoken language. For several years, Broca treated a patient who had been unable to form words and sentences but could understand everything said to him as well as use nonverbal gestures communicate back. When the patient died, Broca performed an autopsy and found a tumor in the lower left frontal cortex. This area is known as *Broca's area*. Soon afterward, Carl Wernicke (1848–1905) discovered a second area located in the left temporal cortex, *Wernicke's area*, which is specialized to comprehend language. Damage to Broca's area or Wernicke's area leads to a serious condition called aphasia, difficulty in producing or comprehending language.

Another famous case leading to an important discovery is the traumatic accident of Phineas Gage. In 1848, Gage worked for the railroad and while he was packing an explosive into a rock, the charge exploded shooting a 3-foot, 13-pound rod through his lower left jaw and out the middle top of his head. Although he lived, his personality was markedly changed. Before the accident he had been known as a quiet, well-mannered man, who worked hard and was conscientious. While Gage was able to walk, talk, and he struggled to make rational decisions, and to regulate emotions, after the accident he was easily irritable, often indecisive and irresponsible. This unfortunate accident provided new opportunity to examine how a specific area of the brain affects particular mental activities. Specifically, this was the first case in which scientists could examine the effect of the frontal lobe on emotional regulation, planning, and decision making. Psychology benefited by discovering the important role of the frontal lobe and the subcortical structures below it on human emotional regulation and motivation. As more research demonstrated that particular areas of the brain produce and influence specific observable behaviors, the dualism perspective lessened. These early studies, along with the ones that followed, helped psychologists to better understand human reactions and the biological influences underlying behaviors. Experimental research in psychology continued to have a strong physiological element; however, the emphasis was primarily on human or animal sensory interactions in response to the environment.

Multiple-Choice Questions

20. Which of the following is a condition in which brain damage results in difficulty in producing or comprehending language?
    (A) Aphasia
    (B) Schizophrenia
    (C) Autism
    (D) Dyslexia

21. Which of the following people was not key in connecting physiology with psychology?
    (A) Francis Galton
    (B) Johannes Müller
    (C) Franz Joseph Gall
    (D) Paul Broca

22. Research on the brain helped move psychology away from the
_____ perspective.

(A) evolution
(B) nativist
(C) dualist
(D) empiricist

23. _____ discovered that the lower left frontal cortex has an
area specific for spoken language.

(A) Francis Galton
(B) Johannes Müller
(C) Franz Joseph Gall
(D) Paul Broca

24. Gall discovered that the brain is made up of _____
unmyelinated and _____ myelinated matter.

(A) pink, white
(B) hot, cold
(C) gray, white
(D) thick, thin

25. The area of the brain that specializes in language comprehension is
located in

(A) the left temporal cortex
(B) the left occipital lobe
(C) the prefrontal cortex
(D) Broca's area

26. Carl Wernicke discovered that damage to the left temporal cortex resulted
in impaired language comprehension. This area is known as

(A) the corpus colosseum
(B) Wernicke's area
(C) the hypothalamus
(D) Broca's area

Fill-in-the-Blank Questions

27. The study of biological processes, especially in the human body, is called _____.

28. Research on sensory thresholds sets the stage for ongoing study of the _____.

29. When a particular area of the brain is stimulated, a/an _____ response occurs.

30. The theory that specific mental abilities, characteristics, and a variety of psychological functions are localized in specific regions of the brain is called _____.

31. _____ asserted that the bumps and indentations of the brain, and their sizes, reflected the strength or weakness of the brain.

32. The area in the left frontal lobe associated with spoken language is known as _____.

33. Damage to the left temporal cortex can lead to language comprehension difficulties. This area is known as _____.

Short-Answer Questions

34. Explain how by examining the brains of deceased patients with brain damage, researchers were able to demonstrate a connection between mental processes (the mind) and the body (the brain).

35. Explain the practice of phrenology.

36. How did the case of Phineas Gage contribute to psychology?

37. Describe what Paul Broca learned about language processing after performing an autopsy on his deceased patient's brain.

38. Describe the important role physiology had in promoting psychology as a science.

Structuralism and Functionalism

Psychological research during much of the 1800s was oriented around the study of mental sensations to physical stimuli. The science of structuralism focused on defining the mind-body connection as sensory threshold responses to external stimuli. Researchers introduced absolute and differential threshold concepts and studied reaction times to explain consciousness.

Wilhelm Wundt, Hermann von Helmholtz, and Edward Titchener were key players in the structuralism movement. Wilhelm Wundt (1832–1920) established psychology in the academic realm by teaching the first formal university-level psychology class and creating the first academic laboratory for psychological research. His early research focused on the thoughts and feelings of conscious experiences and became known as structuralism. During this time Hermann von Helmholtz (1821–1894) created a way to test nerve impulses to explore thresholds and reaction times. Sensory responses were observed and recorded using introspection, the narrated perception of the experience by the individual. Edward Titchener (1867–1927), a student of Wundt, established methods to describe and measure conscious experiences. Titchener focused on identifying the mental elements or the qualities of the conscious sensory experiences. These researchers, though still on the quest to discover the relationship between the mind and body, helped to establish psychology as an experimental science. Structuralism, as a science, did not last long because of the inconsistencies in interpretations of experiences. It was soon realized that defining conscious experience by elements was likely impossible.

Influential researchers such as William James (1842–1910), John Dewey (1859–1952), John James Rowland Angell (1869–1949), and others asserted that each element has a functional role, or a purpose in the experience, which became the science known as functionalism. The function of conscious experience was thought to promote survival through learning and instinctive reactions. Functionalism quickly became the new American philosophy, published in American psychology textbooks and taught in higher education settings.

Wundt and Titchener did not agree with the new functionalist approach to psychology because it was not an experimental psychology. In addition, themes of evolution underlay James's, Dewey's, and Angell's perspectives. James's research emphasized the individual interacting in the natural setting; Dewey highlighted the effect of the experience on the organism as a reaction to a particular stimulus; and Angell proposed that the purpose of psychology was to explore how the mind influences adaptive behaviors. Each progressed the idea of the functional relationship between the mental processes and adaptive behaviors as the individual interacts in the environment, but Dewey and Angell were instrumental in bringing greater understanding of how human behaviors change in response to experiences. Functionalism emphasized the individual responses to stimulus and incorporated learning with adaptive behaviors, and in many ways established the foundation on which subsequent psychological schools of thought could develop.

Researchers such as Wundt, James, Dewey, and Angell made significant contributions toward establishing psychology as a science and introduced it to the academic setting. Early courses were taught from experimental, structuralist, or functionalist perspectives. Sensory reflexes and conscious experiences helped researchers such as Titchener identify elemental qualities of experiences. Stimulus and reactions to it led to exploration of how the individual adapts behaviors based on outcomes. Still it is important to understand how early philosophical roots contributed to what we know about human behaviors today. Equally important is to realize that psychology is continually adapting as physiological and sociological perspectives evolve.

Multiple-Choice Questions

39. Which of the following people was not instrumental in advancing the structuralist movement within psychology?

(A) Wilhelm Wundt
(B) William James
(C) Hermann von Helmholtz
(D) Edward Titchener

40. _____ established the first psychology lab in 1879.

(A) Wilhelm Wundt
(B) William James
(C) Hermann von Helmholtz
(D) Edward Titchener

41. Researchers within the structuralist perspective were trained in _____ as a way to break down experiences into elemental qualities.

(A) inner forces
(B) introspection
(C) observation
(D) perception

42. _____ taught the first formal university-level psychology class.

(A) Wilhelm Wundt
(B) William James
(C) Hermann von Helmholtz
(D) Edward Titchener

43. _____ was the first educator in psychology in Germany, while _____ was the first educator in psychology in the United States.
    (A) Wilhelm Wundt, William James
    (B) William James, Edward Titchener
    (C) Wilhelm Wundt, Hermann von Helmholtz
    (D) Edward Titchener, Hermann von Helmholtz

44. Structuralism defined the mind-body connection as _____ responses to external stimuli.
    (A) adaptation
    (B) mental quality
    (C) sensory threshold
    (D) reflection

45. _____ discounted breaking experiences into elements and focused more on the importance of the interactions of the organism in the natural setting.
    (A) Functionalism
    (B) Nativism
    (C) Empiricism
    (D) Structuralism

Fill-in-the-Blank Questions

46. Wilhelm Wundt's approach focusing on uncovering the fundamental mental components of consciousness, thinking, and other kinds of mental activities is called _____.

47. Researchers within the structuralist perspective were highly interested in the _____, or the amount of time it takes an organism to respond to a particular stimulus.

48. Using one's own words to interpret the experience of eating a crisp red apple is using the structuralism procedure _____.

49. Functionalism disagreed with breaking down conscious experiences into the basic elements because _____.

50. Structuralism relied on _____ methodology, while functionalism relied primarily on _____ methodology.

51. John Dewey focused on what was _____ by experience and how it influenced _____ experiences with the same stimulus.

52. James Rowland Angell emphasized understanding the relationships between the mental processes of an organism as it interacts in its environment and the adaptive behaviors that promote _____.

Short-Answer Questions

53. Explain how functionalist and structuralist researchers advanced understanding of how the mind works and the connection between the mind and body.

54. What were some of the limitations of structuralism?

55. Functionalist and structuralist perspectives defined psychology as the science of conscious experiences. In what ways did functionalism differ from structuralism?

56. Describe some of the academic contributions of structuralism to psychology.

57. Explain how William James helped bring psychology's focus to the adaptive nature of consciousness.

Evolution

Evolutionary theorists explored how and why organisms changed over time, noting that changes were both biological and behavioral. Evolutionary psychology assumes that human behavior is handed down through millions of years of natural selection. Behaviors that are largely detrimental today such as the stress response, aggression, or preference for high-fat foods were once adaptive in the environment of our ancestors. The quick and effective stress response ensured our ancestors were more likely to escape life-threatening dangers. Furthermore, the most aggressive in acquiring food and securing sexual partners were the ones who lived and passed on their genes. Also when food was scarce, those who had a preference for high-fat foods obtained the calories needed to survive.

Adaptation was the heart of evolutionary theory. Researchers such as Charles Darwin (1809–1882) and Francis Galton (1822–1911) were influential in laying a foundation for functionalist psychology. They found that modifications such as changes in food consumption patterns to adapt to availability, or changes in pigment color patterns to blend into a changing environmental color scheme, allowed the organism to live long enough to reproduce and protect offspring. In addition, these adaptations began showing up naturally in offspring, demonstrating that acquired elemental qualities could be passed on through heredity. Darwin considered biological adaptation, which ensured survival of the species and occasionally led to creating a new species entirely, the basic principle of natural selection. Evolutionary psychology holds that natural selection is the preservation of mental and behavioral adaptions that ensure survival of the organism and the species.

Darwin's research was both widely accepted and deeply rejected. In many ways, his origin of species research challenged the dominant perspective of creationism. Where creationism emphasized God's creation of all living things, Darwin found evidence that through ongoing adaptation to changing environmental demands, the species themselves evolved to the point of becoming a distinctively new species. Darwin's research was well documented, very detailed, and relied on scientific methods to measure observable changes. Functional psychology adopted Darwin's scientific observational methods, along with some of his findings surrounding adaptation. However, Darwin was not the only evolutionary researcher to contribute to psychology.

Francis Galton's research extended knowledge of individual differences, which was lightly touched on by the structuralist perspective. Galton explored heredity, specifically within accomplished circles. Without discounting environmental influences such as opportunities and observational learning, Galton proposed that people could evolve to their greatest potential by selective breeding, which led him to found eugenics science. Qualities such as physically beautiful features, high levels of testosterone, youth, and fertility are universally attractive. Attraction from the evolutionary perspective holds that people should naturally be attracted to others with the genetic parental tendencies and qualities that will enable offspring to develop and grow and become parents themselves and thereby continue survival of the species. Masculine features are associated with testosterone levels and frequently accompanied by strength. From an evolutionary perspective, a strong male has increased opportunity for mate selection, and increases the chance of survival for offspring. Similarly, immature feminine features are associated with estrogen, nurturing, and fertility in women and are desirable to men for reproduction. Furthermore, each gender has a shape preference. Women prefer male bodies with broad shoulders and a narrowed waist, or the shape of an inverted triangle. Likewise, males have a strong preference for females with an hourglass shape, or broad shoulders, small waist, and broad hips. Any physical or behavioral feature that increases the likelihood of reproduction falls within the natural selection perspective.

From the evolutionary perspective, it is clear that all of the conscious and unconscious sensations and responses are important and relevant to experiences and the resulting outcome. Darwin's evolutionary findings highlighted how the organism actively promotes its survival through adapting to changes in the environment. Galton's research on individual differences introduced psychology to scientific methods for studying human behaviors. His significant contributions to psychology were in his methodology for quantifying and analyzing psychological elements, or traits.

Multiple-Choice Questions

58. _____ is the preservation of mental and behavioral adaptions that ensure survival of the organism and the species.

(A) Natural selection
(B) Consumption pattern
(C) Pigment color
(D) Evolution

59. Darwin's theory of _____ plays a prominent role in psychology today.

(A) dualism
(B) functionalism
(C) nativism
(D) evolution

60. According to Darwin, _____ was essential for survival of the species.

(A) learning
(B) adaptation
(C) creation
(D) pigment color

61. At the time Darwin proposed it, the evolutionary perspective was considered contradictory to

(A) structuralism
(B) functionalism
(C) creationism
(D) evolution

62. Francis Galton asserted that people could evolve to their greatest potential by _____.

(A) selective breeding
(B) creationism
(C) nativism
(D) evolution

63. Attraction, according to the evolutionary perspective, may be nature's way of letting us know a person has the genetic potential for
_____.
    (A) selective breeding
    (B) parental tendencies
    (C) creationism
    (D) evolution

64. Galton's research on individual differences introduced psychology to _____ for studying human behaviors.
    (A) the scientific method
    (B) introspection
    (C) adaptation
    (D) evolution

Fill-in-the-Blank Questions

65. The psychological approach emphasizing that the mind is a collection of the preserved mental and behavioral adaptions that allow us to overcome problems that our ancestors faced over millions of years is _____.

66. Evolutionary psychology holds that an organism changes both biologically and _____ over time.

67. Modifications such as changes in food consumption patterns to adapt to availability or changes in pigment color patterns to blend into a changing environmental color scheme are examples of _____.

68. The tendency to like sweet foods may have a/an _____ basis that promoted survival during times when the foods that had the highest nutritional value were fruits.

69. Men are most attracted to women who have a/an _____ shape, whereas women find the inverted _____ shape most attractive in men.

70. Darwin and Galton were key in introducing the evolutionary perspective to psychology, and both made many contributions to bringing the _____ to psychology.

Short-Answer Questions

71. An evolutionary perspective holds that jealousy aids in reproduction. Explain this perspective.

72. In what ways does evolutionary psychology affect psychology today?

73. Explain how changes in food consumption patterns or pigment color patterns can ensure survival of a species.

74. Explain why according to the evolutionary psychology perspective natural selection can be applied to explain our mate selection behaviors.

75. Explain how behaviors that are harmful today, such as aggression, acute stress, and high-fat diets, were once essential in the survival of our species.

CHAPTER 2

Nature versus Nurture: Perspectives on Individual Differences

Genes and Heredity

The nature versus nurture debate has been underway for a very long time, and behaviors and risk associated with genetic predisposition and heredity are still being explored. In 2003, the Human Genome Project completed its efforts to sequence and map all the genes involved in developing into a human being. Thanks to the Human Genome Project and genome mapping, genetic risk can be detected and often isolated to the gene or genes involved in risk. However, researchers are still exploring why some genes express while others do not.

The human genome is the complete set of molecular instructions to create a human being, and each person, with the exception of monozygotic twins, has a unique genotype at birth. Within each human cell are 46 chromosomes, with the exception of the gametes or reproductive cells, the sperm and ova, in which there are 23 chromosomes. Chromosomes contain strands of deoxyribonucleic acid (DNA), which are asymmetrically bound together by specific combinations among four proteins, adenine (A), thymine (T), guanine (G), and cytosine (C), to form a double helix shape. The proteins bind as either AT, TA, GC or CG, and combinations occur as sections of the DNA strand according to the particular development goal. Each section of DNA is a gene responsible for passing on heredity, or expressing a particular trait and characteristic.

Behavioral genetics studies the effects of heredity on behavior, and molecular genetics seeks to identify genes associated with specific behaviors. Identifying and understanding expression of genes associated with a behavior or disorder helps scientists learn how to treat or prevent the disorder or disease. Genetic and chromosomal abnormalities can have a profound effect on an individual's development. Chromosome abnormalities result in a particular syndrome such as Down syndrome, a condition in which a zygote receives an extra X chromosome at conception; and Turner's syndrome, a condition in which female infants have only one X chromosome. Genetic disorders may be dominant, requiring a single gene to express, or recessive, requiring a gene from both parents to express. Phenylketonuria (PKU) is a recessive genetic disorder interfering with digestion of protein that can be treated if detected early, whereas Tay-Sachs disease, a recessive genetic disease that causes an enzyme deficiency, is a fatal childhood disease that cannot be treated even when caught early. Recessive genetic disorders outnumber dominant disorders, even though only a single gene is required to express dominant disorders, because many dominant disorders are fatal in childhood and not passed on, whereas recessive genes are carried and frequently passed on to offspring.

The human phenotype is the heredity that we can see, including physical traits such as eye color, as well as many behavioral traits, such as personality. A gene can be dominant or recessive based on the likelihood of phenotype expression. For example, there is a greater chance for brown-eyed children if one of the parents has brown eyes, regardless of the other parent's eye color. Brown is the dominant eye color since only one gene allele is necessary to express it. The genes for blue and green eyes are recessive—often present but not expressed because both parents must pass blue genes to a child in order for the blue eye color to show. Phenotypes are both polygenetic and multifactorial, meaning that the interactions of many genes, as well as many environmental influences before and after the birth of a child, can influence observable traits.

Genotype helps explain similarities among families. For example, twin studies find many similarities between twins raised apart in regard to potential and abilities, even though the environments were not the same. It is not surprising that in many cases, twins raised apart still work in similar jobs and have similar hobbies and interests. On the other hand, environmental influences can change genotype potential. Interpersonal qualities, especially self-constructs, are unique among siblings, including twins raised in the same environment. Although phenotypes of twin siblings are not exactly the same, there is a greater similarity on personality traits in identical twins than other types of siblings. Environmental interactions and experiences are usually the reason for varying degrees of differences in trait expression.

At conception, the combined gametes of the two parents become a zygote containing 46 chromosomes containing the DNA to develop a human offspring. At conception, the combination of (Y) and/or (X) on the twenty-third chromosome determines the gender. An XY chromosome pair results in a male, and XX chromosomes result in a female. Gender is determined by the father's gametes, which as a male can contain either an X or a Y chromosome. Given that each parent provides around 10,000 genes to each child, there are millions of variations as to which genes are inherited. Identical or monozygotic twins share exactly the same DNA because they originate from the same gametes. Other siblings, including fraternal or dizygotic twins, originate from different gamete pairs, and therefore each has a unique genome.

Heredity cannot explain everything about a person, nor can it account for all the similarities and differences among people in the same family, including twins. The risk and protective influences on human behavior and health status are both polygenetic and multifactorial. No two people will experience the same events, environmental influence, or genetic trait expressions in exactly the same way. An amalgamation of genes predispose humans to behave in particular ways in response to external or environmental influences.

Multiple-Choice Questions

76. An organism's entire genetic inheritance is referred to as its

    (A) gamete
    (B) genome
    (C) zygote
    (D) genotype

77. Monozygotic twins are also known as

    (A) half-siblings
    (B) identical twins
    (C) phenotypical twins
    (D) fraternal twins

78. Marsha has twins, a boy and a girl. The twins are

    (A) half-siblings
    (B) identical twins
    (C) phenotypical twins
    (D) dizygotic twins

79. In genetic terms, if you are a "carrier" it means you have

    (A) recessive genes in your genotype that are not expressed
    (B) dominant genes in your phenotype that are expressed
    (C) dominant genes in your phenotype that are not expressed
    (D) dominant genes in your genotype that are expressed

80. When considering the influence of genes on behaviors, disorders, and diseases, it is important to remember that

    (A) heritability dominates environmental influences
    (B) genes are not destiny
    (C) genes determine behaviors
    (D) DNA determines outcomes

81. The twenty-third chromosome pair determines
    (A) genotype
    (B) phenotype
    (C) gender
    (D) eye color

Fill-in-the-Blank Questions

82. A characteristic that is determined by many genes is called _____; one that is the result of the interaction of many genetic and environmental factors is called _____.

83. The _____ questions the degree to which environment and heredity influence human behaviors.

84. Examining genetic markers associated with expression of diseases such as breast cancer is the type of research conducted by the _____.

85. Each cell of the human body contains ____ chromosomes, except for the reproductive cells, which contain _____ chromosomes.

86. _____ contains the genes responsible for passing on heredity, or expressing a particular trait or characteristic.

87. The human genome is the complete set of molecular instructions to create a human life form, and each person (except identical twins) has a unique _____.

88. The role of the proteins of DNA is to combine and form the building blocks of _____.

89. The visible characteristic of gene expression is called the _____.

Short-Answer Questions

90. Describe the relationship between an individual's genotype and phenotype.

91. Explain the difference between a dominant and a recessive gene on the phenotype.

92. Jason and Tiffany, the proud parents of Matthew, were surprised that Matthew has blue eyes, because both of them and both sets of grandparents have brown eyes. Explain how Matt could have blue eyes when both of his parents and his grandparents have brown eyes.

93. Bryan and Ryan are 17-year-old identical twins. Ryan has recently discovered he has a strong interest and clear talent for playing soccer. Bryan finds soccer too challenging and is more interested in creative dance. Both twins are pursuing their interest while in high school and are planning to continue doing so when they begin college after graduation. How can genetics explain the similarities and differences in their talents?

94. Explain why recessive genetic disorders outnumber dominant disorders. Give an example.

Temperament

Temperament, a term, used to describe and classify emotional-behavioral traits, can be detected as early as infancy. Efforts to understand temperament date back to the Greek philosophers Hippocrates (the four humors, see Chapter 1) and Galen (AD 130–200), who first attempted to classify temperament physiologically using elemental qualities: warm, cold, moist, and dry. Galen believed temperament was a result of having a dominant humor as well as the unique combination of the humors. Based on this combination, temperament could be classified as being sanguine, choleric, melancholic, and phlegmatic. Each temperament category presents a characteristic or trait expression. A sanguine temperament is associated with being outgoing and optimistic, choleric is associated with anger and hostility, melancholic is associated with lethargy and unhappiness, and phlegmatic is associated with calmness. Within this theory, the balance among the four bodily fluids, or humors, was not regulated merely by the body, but also by seasons, foods, and herbs. Persian scholars first introduced psychological aspects into temperament, and by the 1600s temperament was commonly associated with personality.

Much of what is known about temperament in traditional U.S. practice is based on the *New York Longitudinal Study* by Alexander Thomas and Stella Chess (as cited in Broderick & Blewitt, 2003, pp. 139–141). Infant reactivity is distinguished across four types of temperament: difficult, easy, slow to warm up, and hard to classify. While some children are hard to classify, most, two-thirds or more, will fit into one of the other three categories. Approximately 40 percent of children have an easy temperament. They are easily comforted, more often content and relaxed, and are typically easy to keep on schedule. On the other hand, around 15 percent of children have a slow-to-warm-up temperament. They also tend to be easier to keep on schedule and are quite content; however, they also have higher levels of fearfulness. Last, about 10 percent of children have difficult temperaments, and are hard to comfort. They have high fearfulness, become irritable easily, and may be in general overly restless.

Temperament is mostly enduring; however, behavior associated with temperament can be modified over a life span in response to stress and reinforcements. Naturally, there are variances within each of the categories depending on the degree of trait expression. Nine traits are used to classifying temperaments: activity level, rhythmicity or regularity, approach/withdrawal, adaptability, sensory threshold, intensity, mood, distractibility, and persistence and attention span. In looking closely at each trait, it may be clear that a trait can be both desirable and undesirable at times. For example, perseverance is necessary to learn how to tie one's shoe; however, persistently asking for a piece of candy in the store creates a problem. Something similar might be said for sensory threshold, where high response to touch could be a calming state for one baby, yet stressful to another. In this example, both might be high responders, yet the corresponding behaviors are very different.

The degree of trait expression provides understanding for classifying a baby as either difficult, easy, or slow to warm up using a scale rating system in which each parent marks where the child's emotional/behavioral patterns fall on the spectrum. Regarding persistence and attention span, for example, one polar description includes "sticks with a task until completed, or does not give up easily." Whereas the opposing polar end description is, "fails to complete tasks, and gives up easily." Importantly, this scaling technique only provides insights to the child's temperament tendencies. The bigger picture also requires understanding of the parent's temperament patterns.

Temperament patterns tend to be permanent, and over time, emotional and behavioral experiences reinforce how we express them. A child with greater persistence and a long attention span may be successful in learning how to place shapes in the correct sorter slot, but may be considered stubborn when persistently attempting to play with a shiny tree ornament. The same child may ignore distractions in class long enough to complete school assignments, but may "stubbornly" insist on doing homework after playing with friends. Persistence continues to support or inhibit reaching goals throughout life; however, early parental responses to childhood perseverance are equally influential.

Goodness of fit between parent and child temperaments determines caregiver responses, influences a child's problem-solving style, and sets the stage for patterns in other relationships. Parents with a difficult temperament are more likely to struggle with a child of difficult temperament, and they may not be able to allow the time the child needs to resolve challenges. Parents who are easily distracted and irritated by uncooperative or ambitious children may lack patience and empathy for the child. Ongoing strict, demanding, or impatient parenting styles may inhibit creative growth, disrupt healthy emotional regulation, or spark rebellion in a child, whereas having an easy temperament will help the parent be patient in allowing the child to learn how to overcome problems.

The relationship dynamics between a parent and child also shape behaviors and expectations the child has about other interpersonal relationships. For example, the persistent child who forces goal attainment through rebellion, disregard to rules, or because the parents give up enforcing the rules may not learn valuable lessons about pride for accomplishment or attaining goals through mutual cooperation, collaboration, and teamwork. These children may become demanding adolescents and adults with unrealistic expectations of other people. They may behave in ways that strain friendships, and when others do not give in to their demands, experience a great deal of disappointment.

Temperament plays a key role in coping and problem solving in both the parent and the child. Just as easy temperament parents can adapt their approach with a difficult child, an easy child can find a niche with parents of difficult temperaments. Similarly, two siblings will have different childhood experiences though raised by the same parents. Parents respond to each child differently, and children tend to create their own worlds wherever they are. However, problems arise when a goodness of fit cannot be achieved.

Because both parent and child influence the relationship dynamics, emotional and behavioral characteristics of the child affect the parent in ways that establish attitudes about the nature of the child. Parents come to expect children to behave in particular ways, and children do the same with the parents. When a parent has a negative attitude and expects the child to fail in gaining approval or reaching a desired goal, a child may become anxious and defensive and develop behavioral problems. Likewise, parents can become avoidant in reproaching children that become overly sensitive or hostile. The effect of goodness of fit on a child's development is typically noticeable in the home, social, and academic settings.

Multiple-Choice Questions

95. Individual differences in emotions, activity, and self-control are referred to as one's

(A) affect
(B) personality
(C) temperament
(D) coping style

96. Temperament can shift by degrees but will not drastically change over one's life span because

(A) temperament is determined by heredity
(B) temperament is a result of parenting style
(C) temperament is fixed at adulthood
(D) temperament is a result of nature and nurture

97. According to the _____, temperament can be classified into four categories.

    (A) Seattle Longitudinal Study
    (B) New York Institute of Research
    (C) National Institute of Health
    (D) New York Longitudinal Study

98. Which of the following is not a temperament category?

    (A) Pleasant
    (B) Difficult
    (C) Easy
    (D) Hard to Classify

99. Temperament behaviors among toddlers are more likely to persist when reinforced by parents. Which of the following children's temperament is most likely to change?

    (A) A child who is fearful and inhibited
    (B) A child who is easygoing and exuberant
    (C) A child who is irritable and unpredictable
    (D) A child who is balanced in positivity and fearfulness

100. Marcus is a four-month-old boy who is mostly content and playful. His mother has few challenges in keeping him on schedule; however, he startles easily, which suggests he may have some fearful reactions. Which temperament category is Marcus most likely to be classified under?

    (A) Hard to classify
    (B) Easy
    (C) Slow to warm up
    (D) Difficult

101. _____ is the dynamics between the parent and child temperaments.

    (A) Goodness of fit
    (B) Synchrony
    (C) Persistence
    (D) Reactivity

Fill-in-the-Blank Questions

102. According to the New York Longitudinal Study, by approximately three months of age, infants exhibit _____ temperamental traits.

103. Slow to warm up is one of the four categories of temperament suggested by the _____.

104. Temperament traits remain constant for the most part, however, _____ and _____ experiences can reinforce how we express.

105. Galen believed temperament was a result of having a _____ humor as well as the unique _____ of the humors.

106. Children with a/an _____ temperament are easily comforted, more often content, and relaxed, and are typically easy to keep on schedule.

107. To measure a child's temperament, each parent marks on a scale where the child's _____ patterns fall on the spectrum.

108. Temperament is a/an _____ disposition that emerges early in life and tends to be permanent over the course of the life span.

Short-Answer Questions

109. Six months ago, Mark and Ann welcomed their first child, Jason, into their happy home. For the past three months, Jason has become very irregular in his sleeping and eating patterns. He wakes up every two to three hours during the night and does not drink his bottle completely or timely when Ann feeds him. Ann has been gradually increasing her time at work, but has not yet returned to full-time. Jason's changing needs are interfering with her sleep cycle, and she is not eating regularly either. Mark does not seem to be bothered by loss of sleep, and he rotates nights with Ann. Ann is unable to relax and sleep soundly or for more than three or four hours on Mark's nights. She has no appetite when it is time to eat but will snack on sweets through the day because she feels tired. Ann's interactions with Jason have also changed; she does not talk or interact as much, and she does not engage with Jason when she cares for him. Jason seems to eat better and appears to be more content when Mark feeds him. Mark is much better at getting Jason to smile and coo when he interacts. Mark indicated that Jason looks away from Ann when she feeds him, and he does not seem to connect with her in the same playful way.

Which temperament trait categories are most concerning for Jason and Ann?

110. In the situation in Question 109, Ann and Jason have similar temperaments. Rate them as easy or difficult in regard to the following, and explain
your rating:

    Approach/withdrawal: easy/difficult
    Adaptability: easy/difficult
    Rhythmicity: easy/difficult

111. Three-year-old Mark does not like to be held on his mother's lap for very
long. He wiggles and squirms to get down, and he reaches for the things
he finds interesting, many of which he loses interest in quickly. Rate Mark
as easy or difficult on activity level and on persistence and attention span.
Explain your answers.

112. Nine-month-old Lexie is easily startled, becomes fussy at bath time, and
frequently cries when her diaper becomes soiled. She is not easily comforted once she becomes upset and can be tearful for hours at a time. Rate
Lexie as easy or difficult on mood and threshold. Explain your answers.

113. Six-year-old Tyler does very well in his first-grade class. Even though the
child seated next to him talks to him during assignment time, Tyler completes his assignments in full and with very few mistakes. Rate Tyler as
easy or difficult on persistence and attention span, and on distractibility.
Explain your answers.

Personality

Humans have similar characteristics and attributes; however, people are very different from one person to the next. The complex task of describing humans is
primarily done by comparing concrete actions or behaviors to abstract ideas of temperaments. Dating back as far as Hippocrates, theories have been formed to explain
how people differ, and most early physicians asserted that differences were largely
due to individual biology. Initial perspectives grew from the four humors theory,
thought to be an extension of early Egyptians' theory involving the elements air,
fire, earth, and water. Hippocrates thought the body regulated four essential fluids,
blood, yellow bile, black bile, and phlegm, which were responsible for well-being
and health. A prolonged excess or deficiency of any of these fluids could lead
to illness. Galen thought that the fluids worked in combination with each other
to define temperament states, which in turn influenced personality. Imbalances,
according to Galen, could lead to negative personality types.

Early trait theorists such as Gordon Allport (1897–1967) believed that people
could be described in terms of combination of traits much like how an object could
be described by its properties. From early childhood throughout adulthood, there
are consistent patterns of behaviors within a person that can be used to describe,
explain, and predict behaviors. Allport believed that traits remained relatively

stable and that traits presented as a person's disposition, however no behavior can be defined by only one trait. Allport believed that people possess common traits that are shared among a culture, and personal traits that are representative of an individual's disposition or personality. Personality traits are often noticeable by the way people set and achieve their goals, and delay self-gratification in order to avoid a negative consequence. Postponement of something desired, or delaying gratification, triggers a physiological stress response causing varying degrees of discomfort and anxiety. Therefore, ongoing stressors have a negative effect on personality. Raymond Catell (1905–1998) was successful in reducing human traits into a cluster theory of 16 bipolar traits, which he termed source traits. Catell illustrated source traits by characterizing common behaviors and associated occupations. His theory suggested that one's personality is a series of behaviors that fall between two extremes. For example, the high and low titles of the source Factor E are dominance and submissiveness, respectively. Catell noted that people who are humble and accommodating, such as priests or clergy, often score low in Factor E. Likewise, high scores were common in assertive and competitive people such as athletes and researchers. While factor analysis was useful in scientifically narrowing down the many human trait correlations, it is not widely used in today's personality assessments because it centered on subjective natures of instinctive behaviors.

Hans Eysenck (1916–1997) also used factor analysis to explain personality. His theory proposed a three-factor theory in which he believed biology was central to the expression of high or low degrees of arousal and conditioning. He believed the three factors of personality are extraversion, neuroticism, and psychoticism. Extraversion has to do with the aspect of social behaviors, neuroticism relates to emotional stability, and psychoticism relates to irrational thinking. Individuals scoring high on extraversion tend to be active, social, engaging, and thrill seeking. Neuroticism is characterized by anxiousness or depression and general discontent with self and others. Psychoticism is characterized by antisocial behaviors such as aggression, egocentric and impersonal perspectives, and impulsivity. Heredity is an important influence in personality expression in Eysenck's theory; however, he believes that neurotic behaviors are learned or conditioned. While Catell's theory was too complex, Eysenck's theory was too restrictive.

More recent research suggests a five-factor model known as the Big Five personality traits. The factors are commonly referred to as OCEAN and include openness (O), conscientiousness (C), extraversion (E), agreeableness (A), and neuroticism (N). The traits tend to be influenced by experiences through childhood, but are thought to be mostly stable by adulthood. Extraversion and openness tend to decrease with age, whereas agreeableness and conscientiousness increase. Personality has a key role in how people adapt to stress and how flexible they are to change. Neurochemicals dopamine, serotonin, and norepinephrine are associated with behavioral activation, inhibition, and regulation and are linked to the five personality traits. Maladaptive behaviors, antisocial behaviors, and inflexibility are indicative of personality disorders, and they are diagnosed when it becomes difficult for a person to function in expected social roles.

Some personality disorders may be apparent in childhood, while others may develop in adulthood. Childhood antisocial behaviors are not always indicative of a personality disorder; however, when antisocial behaviors are persistent, the child is likely to struggle with authority and rules inside structured settings such as school. Typically, personality disorders are diagnosed in adulthood, although a history of conduct problems in childhood, as well as a less resilient temperament, is common, especially in antisocial disorders.

Personality is measured by self-report or projective methods. Projective measures include the Rorschach Inkblot Test and the Thematic Apperception Test (TAT). Rorschach assessments utilize a series of symmetrical visuals in which individuals view and then describe what the image brings to mind. The Thematic Apperception Test also utilizes pictures; however, instead of a verbalized story, the individual writes a story. Both approaches require a qualified psychologist to interpret characteristics of personality. Because many question the validity and reliability of projection assessments, outside of clinical settings self-report questionnaires are preferred.

The most frequently used self-report personality assessment is the Minnesota Multiphasic Personality Inventory-2 (MMPI-2) (Framingham, 2013), and it is also the most often used to assess for personality disorders in a clinical setting. Through a series of questions, the test finds patterns that may indicate abnormal personality traits indicative of a psychological disorder. It is a psychological tool administered and interpreted by qualified mental health professionals. Other assessments have been useful in creating a personality profile, including the Myers-Briggs Type Indicator (MBTI) (The Myers & Briggs Foundation, 2015) and the Keirsey Temperament Sorter II (Keirsey.com, n.d.). The MBTI and Keirsey Temperament Sorter II are used professionally to assess measures that may be predictive of individual behaviors or decision preferences.

The MBTI profiles personality by identifying patterns of an individual's qualities: interests, needs, values, and motivations, which influence decision-making style. This profile is based on self-perceptions on dichotomies of introversion or extraversion (E); intuition (I) or sensing (S); feeling (F) or thinking (T); and judging (J) or perception (P). Each dichotomy represents an attitude or functional expression of personality. Individual attitudes are highlighted by the extraversion/introversion dichotomy. Each personality type differs on defining characteristics by degrees rather than being an either/or classification. Scoring of the MBTI results is a four-letter code according to dominance, or highest to lowest scores.

The Keirsey Temperament Sorter II most closely resembles the ancient theories of Hippocrates. Personality traits are sorted by temperament qualities and classified by role characteristics into categories: Artisan, Guardian, Idealistic, or Rational. Similar to the MBTI, scoring will indicate an individual's dominant role type. The theory comprehensively subtypes individuals within variant role types, which can be further subtyped by behavior qualities.

Multiple-Choice Questions

114. Distinctive and characteristic patterns of thought, emotion, and behavior that define an individual's personal style of interacting with the physical and social environment are called

(A) rhythmicity
(B) personality
(C) temperament
(D) humors

115. Which is not one of the four humors proposed by Hippocrates?

(A) Blood
(B) Phlegm
(C) Water
(D) Bile

116. According to Raymond Catell, a person scoring low on source Factor E has a _____ personality.

(A) submissive
(B) completive
(C) dominant
(D) conscientiousness

117. Which of the following was a trait psychologist?

(A) Raymond Catell
(B) Francis Galton
(C) Hippocrates
(D) Abraham Maslow

118. The three factors of personality proposed by Hans Eysenck are

(A) water, metal, fire
(B) conscientiousness, openness, and extraversion
(C) extraversion, neuroticism, and psychoticism
(D) bile, blood, and phlegm

119. Which of the following is not a Big Five factor of personality?

(A) Openness
(B) Conscientiousness
(C) Psychoticism
(D) Neuroticism

120. Which of the following is not used to measure or assess personality?
    (A) Rorschach Inkblot Test
    (B) Thematic Apperception Test (TAT)
    (C) Minnesota Multiphasic Personality Inventory-2 (MMPI-2)
    (D) OCEAN

Fill-in-the-Blank Questions

121. Hippocrates and Galen believed that imbalances in one or more of the essential bodily fluids _____ influenced personality.

122. Allport believed that personality resulted from a combination of _____ which remained relative stable but could be influenced by culture and the environment.

123. To understand personality differences, psychologists are interested in _____, _____, and _____ experiences and events.

124. Raymond Catell believed personality is defined by where an individual falls on the spectrum of 16 _____ source traits.

125. Personality is _____ when behaviors interfere with ability to function in expected social roles.

126. Dopamine is a/an _____ associated with pleasure-seeking behaviors and motivation to work toward a rewarding goal.

127. _____ and _____ are examples of projection assessments.

Short-Answer Questions

128. Describe the influence of heritability on personality according to Eysenck.

129. Explain the influence of nature and nurture on personality.

130. Describe the trait approach to understanding personality.

131. Describe how achieving goals can have a positive and a negative effect on personality.

132. Explain the role of neurochemicals on maladaptive personality expression.

133. Explain the purpose of the Minnesota Multiphasic Personality Inventory-2 (MMPI-2).

Environment

Environment includes all external influences, and it plays a key role in achieving genetic potential. In addition to biology, everything external of the child from conception forward influences development. The external environment includes physical and psychosocial influences. Beginning with conception, there are critical periods of prenatal development that are vulnerable to harmful external agents. A critical period is a time when specific kinds of growth must take place if the embryo is going to develop normally. External influences that have a negative influence on prenatal development are called teratogens and include drugs, chemicals, viruses, and other external factors that cause birth defects.

Pregnancy lasts for about 38 weeks and is broken down into three main periods of development. The germinal period lasts for the first two weeks, during which time there is rapid cell division and the early beginnings of cell differentiation. The third week and lasting through the eighth week is the embryonic period, a critical period for body structures development. The fetal period begins at the ninth week and lasts until birth. During this time sex organs develop and body systems begin functioning. At 22 weeks, the brain is developed to a point that a preterm infant could survive; however, each day after this age of viability, the chances of survival increase significantly. Teratogen exposure at any point during these three periods can result in a physical, cognitive, or behavioral abnormality. Importantly, many teratogens have a threshold effect and may not interfere with development unless the threshold is reached. The challenge in determining a threshold is that it is different from one person to the next.

In addition to teratogens, social supports and social economic status (SES) contribute much to human growth, development, achievement, and health across the life span. The psychosocial environment includes parents, members within the community, culture, additional family members, and friends. Ecological models help organize and identify social supports and the potential contribution or deficit that may be associated with each support. Urie Bronfenbrenner (1917–2005) described three levels of social support surrounding an individual. The first level, microsystem, includes those within the immediate surroundings, such as family and friends. The second level, the exosystem, consists of the various institutions in which the individual interacts, such as churches, schools, and work settings. The third level, macrosystem, includes the cultural values, economic policies, and political processes. Each system is connected to the other and provides resources and vulnerabilities causing instability for an individual. As people grow older, historical experiences and learning become a source of inner support. Likewise, tragic events in the course of one's life have a historical effect on a person as well. Bronfenbrenner refers to this fourth level of support as a chronosystem, acknowledging that the patterns of transitions and opportunities over the course of one's life influence stability and well-being.

Family systems promote healthy development by providing basic necessities, promoting learning, fostering self-respect, cultivating friendships, and promoting stability and harmony. Family structure tends to influence family function by way of resource availability. For example, the nuclear family (with two biological or adoptive parents) most often can provide the greatest financial and biopsychosocial resources. By comparison, single parents often need to pull from one resource to cover another. Regardless of the structure, families that do not support all of their members are considered dysfunctional. Three factors that increase the likelihood of a family to become dysfunctional are low income, low stability, and low harmony. Occasional bouts of conflict between family members are common and have the potential to model cooperation and problem solving. Unfortunately, around half of the marriages in the United States end in divorce, and risk of family instability increases with divorce. Single-parent homes tend to have fewer biopsychosocial resources necessary for a stable environment. However, the structure of a family is less important on childhood resilience than is how the family functions.

Oftentimes children can still find a support niche among friends and others outside the immediate family if the family environment fails to support one or more of the function areas. Having a niche is especially protective for coping with stress and overcoming hardships. In addition, a niche is beneficial when the immediate family environment is unable to support the individual's interests, talents, and goal pursuits. Each support provides a unique learning experience and knowledge resource. Bronfenbrenner termed the dynamic interactions between these systems the mesosystem, a fifth level of support.

Friendships account for the most important relationships for the majority of people. The peer culture provides an essential environment for developing self-concept, self-esteem, and identity. With age, friendships become increasingly more influential in achieving a sense of belonging. Friendships are based on qualities such as trustworthiness, cooperation, fairness, kindness, and become the most important relationships as early as middle childhood. Close friendships provide acceptance, approval, and support beginning in adolescence. Adult support networks are vast and exist in natural settings, such as friendly encounters with members in the community or work colleagues; however, close friendships continue to be among the most important relationships.

Social supports may be the most protective factor for health and wellness, and a breakdown in social supports is the most common cause of stress. Resilience among children and adults is greatly dependent upon how many social supports are in place. Low-income children and other vulnerable population groups do better in all areas when adequate wraparound services are given. Older adults are also vulnerable to insufficient social supports and are found to have fewer biopsychosocial resources than any other age group. Longer life spans mean many more years of declining physical and cognitive abilities. As declines create more problems in performing daily activities, older adults are less able to get out into their communities. Having fewer opportunities for social engagement can reduce the number and strength of the older adult's social networks. Spouses and partners provide a give-and-take support system that protects against frailty; however, loss of spouse can be very difficult, especially for men. Women are more likely not to remarry after the death of a spouse, and to have greater support systems than men. Because men are less interdependent outside of marriage, they are less likely to have sufficient support from friends. Fortunately, older adults have more long-term relationships as well as better relationship skills.

Although the social supports within the microsystem have a great deal of influence on the development and well-being of an individual, supports within the macrosystem have a great deal of influence on establishing norms, decision making, and direction of change. Socioeconomic status (SES) and cultural context influence all other aspects including parenting, biological development, and expression of individual differences.

Socioeconomic status refers to income, wealth, occupation, education, and place of residence. Low SES presents disadvantages, limits opportunities, and can negatively affect biopsychosocial development at every age, and money problems are the primary source of stress and family conflict and instability. Low SES negatively affects the very young and very old more than the population groups in between; however, low income is associated with physical and mental health problems and higher stress, substance abuse, and obesity rates. Furthermore, financial resources influence healthcare resources, and low-income homes tend to have fewer options in regards to healthcare services. Opportunities for education and social engagement may be limited or inaccessible due to lack of funding and demographic location. Often school-based and community social activities require a fee or may not be easily accessible. For many people, participation in social activities influences sense of within and without group belonging. People tend to desire social norms and are influenced by what others are doing. Normative influence has a powerful effect on decisions and behaviors, and on social status within cultural contexts.

The cultural context is made up of individuals who identify as a group sharing the same beliefs and values. Cultural norms establish the social rules for how people within a particular culture should behave in specific situations. Cultural norms are shaped by the various levels or subgroups within the ecological system. Values within a culture can shape perspectives at every group level; however, deviations from the larger culture's values and beliefs are not easily accepted. Often the larger culture must accept and tolerate deviations such as religious beliefs, interracial marriages, divorce, working mothers, and stay-at-home fathers. Culture deviations are harder to accept when they are not understood, are harmful to others, or create dissonance in moral beliefs. Divorce, same-sex relationships, substance use, and abortion are a few examples. Unfortunately, deviating from cultural norms can lead to being rejected by social supports. People without close family supports, adequate interpersonal networks, and resources are at greater risk.

Having developmental challenges, personal incapacities, or values and beliefs different from the primary culture group place people at greater risk. There are often fewer opportunities and more obstacles between them and the basic necessities and supports they need. These disadvantages also raise the risk for poor health and disparity. Vulnerable populations benefit greatly by the social supports at the macrosystem level. Effective environmental systems allocate resources that improve organizations, create relationships, and improve communications and are evaluated on ability to minimize risk and increase outcome potential. Advocates help to increase cultural awareness and competence, and culturally sensitive programs benefit everyone.

Multiple-Choice Questions

134. Environmental influences on child development include all of the following except

(A) heredity
(B) parenting
(C) schools
(D) culture

135. During a/an _____ specific types of development must take place in order for the normal prenatal development to occur.

(A) heredity
(B) critical period
(C) germinal stage
(D) cell differentiation

136. The time when a preterm newborn might survive outside of the uterus is termed the

(A) low birth weight sensitive period
(B) embryonic period
(C) critical period
(D) age of viability

137. A _____ is any agent or condition that increases risk of prenatal abnormalities.

(A) teratogen
(B) phenotype
(C) placenta
(D) chromosome

138. An ecological systems approach to the study of human development was recommended by

(A) Jean Piaget
(B) Erik Erikson
(C) Sigmund Freud
(D) Urie Bronfenbrenner

139. The first three levels of social support within Urie Bronfenbrenner's ecological model are _____, _____, and _____.

(A) chronosystem, microsystem, macrosystem
(B) exosystem, chronosystem, macrosystem
(C) microsystem, exosystem, macrosystem
(D) mesosystem, microsystem, macrosystem

140. From an ecological systems perspective, the influence of a child's parents on his development is part of his _____, and the influence of his school is part of his _____.

(A) chronosystem, microsystem
(B) exosystem, macrosystem
(C) microsystem, exosystem
(D) mesosystem, microsystem

Fill-in-the-Blank Questions

141. List the three stages of prenatal development in the correct order of occurrence: _____, _____, and _____.

142. The important developmental factor in reaching the age of viability is _____.

143. Developmental psychologists refer to nurture as the influences in the world around us including family, friends, schools, air quality, nutrition, and community, or the _____.

144. The prenatal environment is vulnerable to _____, such as viruses, drugs, and air pollutants.

145. The _____ environment includes family, friends, school, community, demographic location, culture, and other social relationships and resources.

146. Individuals in the same cohort are exposed to the same historical context, which according to the ecological systems is the _____ level of social support.

147. Insufficient income, instability, and disharmony are characteristics of a _____ family.

Short-Answer Questions

148. Describe some of the environmental influences on fetal development.

149. Explain the importance of a critical period of development.

150. Describe the first three levels of the ecological model according to Urie Bronfenbrenner.

151. Explain how the events within the chronosystem can have a positive influence as well as a negative influence on an individual's development.

152. Which is more important for childhood reliance, family structure or family functioning? Why?

153. Discuss some of the protective and risk factors of socioeconomic status on development.

154. Explain why friendships are often the most important relationships for people.

Parenting

Understanding of an individual's temperament and personality are valuable in relating to behavior motivations and barriers; however, people do not exist in a vacuum. Family units consist of many unique temperaments and personalities. Each person within any family unit has a unique interpersonal experience that works to shape the type of independent person he or she becomes in life. The influence of parenting can be best understood by understanding the importance of attachment and the different parenting styles.

The synchrony of the parent and child relationship during infancy has a long-lasting effect on the psychosocial development of the child. Interactions that involve interpersonal sensitivity for each other's temperaments pave the way for a healthy and secure attachment process for the child with the primary caregiver. Gradually the child will be able to read others' emotions and will learn how to interact appropriately in social settings.

Attachment is the term used to describe the long-lasting bond between a child and another person, usually the primary caregiver. Infants form the healthiest attachments with parents who are responsive, consistent, and sensitive to their needs. The strength of this bond is evident in children by the child's first birthday by how the child seeks proximity, or works to be near the parent, and in how comforted a child is when the parent returns from being away. A healthy attachment is necessary for infants to overcome separation anxiety in a secure and timely manner.

Harry Harlow (1905–1981) studied separation and dependency behaviors and the role of the maternal bond on infants' psychosocial development. Harlow observed that infant monkeys need to have close and physical contact to form an attachment with their mother, and to feel safe and secure. In his research, he also found the source of physical comfort or contact to be more important to feeling safe and secure than the source of food is, when the two are different. Feeling safe and secure provides the confidence in the infant necessary to explore and learn about the surrounding environment. Security and confidence develop from the reliability of the parent, or in the predictability of the parent being there when the infant needs her. In this way, attachment facilitates the infant's ability to adapt to changes in environment as well as changes in care providers.

John Bowlby (1907–1990) and Mary Ainsworth (1913–1999) are two major contributors in explaining attachment and highlighting behaviors indicative of either a secure or an insecure attachment. Bowlby established the attachment theory stating that the child's attachment to the parent is critical for ongoing social and psychological development. Attachment forms through stages of infant and caregiver interactions. The pre-attachment phase is the early months when the infant recognizes the parent's face but is not yet attached. The infant begins to show a preference for the caregiver during the indiscriminate attachment period, and the discriminate attachment period is when the child experiences distress upon separation from the caregiver. Bowlby suggested that later there is a multiple attachment phase in which the child forms attachments to others. These time frames are critical windows when attachment naturally takes place, and forming attachments outside of these times is much more difficult.

Ainsworth expanded on Bowlby's attachment concepts to describe attachment by patterns of behaviors. As Bowlby suggested, Ainsworth agreed that secure infants will gradually spend more time with their attention diverted from their mother. Ainsworth found four patterns of attachment, which she termed secure, avoidant, resistant/ambivalent, and disorganized. The most common approach to measure attachment is the Strange Situation procedure. In this procedure, the mother and child begin in the same strange setting in which there are a variety of toys for the child to play with. In three-minute intervals, the mother leaves, and then returns. Another variation of this experiment may include the addition of a stranger. Ainsworth suggested that most children do have secure attachments. They desire and seek proximity with the mother, and experience some distress when she is out of sight. Upon her return, securely attached infants are comforted by the mother and tend to resume playing soon after.

Insecurely attached infants are not easily comforted upon reuniting with the mother. There are two types of insecure attachments, avoidant and resistant/ambivalent. Infants with avoidant attachments do not seem to mind when the mother leaves their sight and will not usually seek proximity when she returns. It seems as if these infants do not have an emotional need for the mother. Avoidant types of attachments occur when the parent consistently does not respond to the infant's distress or crying. The more distal the parenting approach, the more the infant learns to self-calm, and therefore is more likely to develop an avoidant attachment. Unlike avoidant attachments, infants with resistant/ambivalent attachments are bothered by separation from the mother, however, her return does not provide them the comfort that it does for a securely attached child. This child is likely to be both angry with the mother and in need of her closeness. These attachment behaviors tend to result from inconsistencies in the parent's response to the infant's distress. The parent may at times be prompt and comforting, while at other times neglectful. The last attachment pattern is termed disorganized because the manner in which children respond is unpredictable. The defining characteristic of this type of attachment is that the child may seek proximity through avoidance behaviors, or in ways that are contradictory to being close to the parent.

Children with disorganized or insecure attachments adapt differently to caregiver and environmental changes or inconsistencies. A child with an avoidant attachment pattern might just as easily be comforted by someone other than the parent, even if it is a stranger. As they age, these children are more likely to exhibit externalizing feelings with acting out with negative behaviors when distressed. They tend to have more aggression and hostility in social interactions, and there is a strong correlation to pathology. On the other hand, children with resistant/ambivalent attachment patterns experience much more anxiety and inability to cope with separation and are not easily comforted by others. They are also more likely to internalize feelings when coping with stress.

Attachment remains stable through adolescence and plays a key role in coping and adjusting to significant changes and loss. Many researchers believe that if a secure attachment is not formed by age two, it is not likely to happen. Children with insecure attachments have more difficulties in adjusting to change and therefore are less resilient. They are also more likely to have difficulties in adult relationships due to these early working models.

Adult attachment behaviors are classified by similar behavior patterns and are classified as secure, anxious-preoccupied, dismissive-avoidant, and fearful-avoidant. When adults have secure attachments, they are able to balance interdependence and independence in relationships. They view themselves and others positively and hold a set of working models for healthy relationship behaviors and expectations. Anxious-preoccupied attachment patterns include suspicions and worry; there is an underlying expectation of negative outcomes, and often adults with this attachment style act impulsively on their suspicions and worry. Strong beliefs that one is self-sufficient and does not need close companionships are characteristic of a dismissive-avoidant attachment. Adults with a dismissive-avoidant attachment style have a strong preference for independence and alone time and are more likely to view relationships as not worth the inevitable painful outcome. Adults with a fearful-avoidant attachment style often engage in contradictory behaviors. They want a close relationship, but because they lack trust in their partner, they are likely to feel distressed and uncertain when in a relationship. Often these adults have a low self-worth, and they usually internalize their feelings.

Adults tend to act in ways that produce the dreaded negative outcomes, making adult attachment behaviors difficult to work through. Early attachment working models establish a framework of expectations and behaviors in relationships, and continued reinforcement of insecure attachment models throughout childhood and adolescence strengthens avoidant attachment behaviors in adulthood. It seems clear that a nurturing parenting style is essential for attachment.

Parenting Style

All parents have an idea of the parent role, and can give a definition of a good parent. While there are many overlapping characteristics of a good parent, Diana Baumrind (1927–) found that there are four common dimensions of parenting: expression of warmth, strategies for discipline, communication, and expectations for maturity. Each dimension exists on a high to low continuum, much like temperament. For example, some parents are very affectionate, or high in expression of warmth, while parents who are cold and critical are low in this dimension. Persistent behavior patterns within each dimension indicate a particular parenting style. These patterns influence the child's expectation of the parents' response in the same way children's behavior influences the parents' expectations. There are three classifications of parenting styles: authoritarian, permissive, and authoritative. Each style is classified according to how persistently characteristics fall above or below the midrange on the four dimensions above.

The authoritarian parenting style is characterized by low expressions of warmth, high critical feedback, and inflexibility on high expectations for maturity and obedience. Communication is low, and primarily parent-to-child, and there is an expectation that the child will do what the parent says, because the parent says. Authoritarian parents love their children and expect them to do their best, but usually "best" is defined by the parent. Emotions are rarely expressed except for anger or disappointment when the child makes a mistake, and mistakes are often punished. As a result, children are generally obedient when they are young and fear the parents' disapproval or punishment. Adolescents tend to internalize emotions and be overly self-critical, or they may become rebellious and leave home as soon as they are able to. Overall, children of authoritarian parents report low levels of happiness and have inadequate social competence and low self-esteem.

A defining characteristic of a permissive parenting style is indulging the child's happiness. Like authoritarian parents, permissive parents love their children; however, they differ by being high in expressions of warmth and having low expectations for maturity. Discipline is rarely given, and communication is high on child-to-parent and low on parent-to-child; parents have high responsiveness to the child's demands. Parents may see themselves as the child's friend, or their role as a guide, but not an authority figure. Most of the time permissive parents strive to avoid confrontation and do not implement structure for the child's behaviors or consequences for misbehaviors. Even though the child's demands are consistently met, children of permissive parents are low in happiness and have poor self-control and emotional regulation. As a result, they are less socially competent and struggle to make and keep friends. Because their behaviors are more immature, accepting boundaries for expectations in social settings such as school is challenging for them.

A final parenting style, according to Baumrind, is an authoritative style. Authoritative parents are highly affectionate, but unlike permissive and authoritarian parents, they have high communication between parent and child, instead of from one or the other. Parents with an authoritative style set expectations for maturity and discipline based on each child's developmental abilities. This may seem inconsistent among children within the same family unit; however, due to the high level of communication and expression of warmth, children gain a high level of autonomy. As a result, children develop adequate self-esteem and social competence, and they report higher happiness. They tend to do better in school, are well liked by others, and therefore are more successful in transitioning to adulthood roles.

Based on Baumrind's research, it might seem that authoritative parenting is the best approach and that permissive and authoritarian parenting styles create unhappy, poorly accepted, and resentful young people who struggle to function in the social contexts essential for performing adult roles. There is evidence for greater advantages from a parenting style that is high in warmth and communication, promotes autonomy through appropriate expectations for maturity, and includes child-centered discipline strategies. However, it is important to realize that the individual differences in children influence parenting style as well as determine how resilient the child is under the parenting approach. There is also evidence that long-term outcomes in most cases are dependent upon the ongoing relationship between parent and child in combination with the individual traits of the child as he or she matures. Furthermore, there is a wide range of variation when measured against SES, culture, and ethnicity factors.

Multiple-Choice Questions

155. The synchrony of the parent and child relationship during infancy has a long-lasting effect on the _____ of the child.

    (A) personality traits
    (B) temperament traits
    (C) academic performance
    (D) psychosocial development

156. _____ is the term used to describe the long-lasting bond between a child and another person, usually the primary caregiver.

(A) Synchrony
(B) Temperament
(C) Attachment
(D) Psychosocial development

157. _____ believed infants need to have close and physical contact to form an attachment with their mother, and to feel safe and secure.

(A) John Bowlby
(B) Erik Erikson
(C) John Piaget
(D) John Watson

158. Which of the following is not one of the four patterns of attachment identified by Mary Ainsworth?

(A) Secure
(B) Avoidant
(C) Resistant/ambivalent
(D) Disconnected

159. Which of the follow is not an adult attachment style?

(A) Fearful avoidant
(B) Dismissive-avoidant
(C) Ambivalent-disorganized
(D) Anxious-preoccupied

160. Which of the following is not a classification of parenting styles?

(A) Authoritarian
(B) Dismissive
(C) Authoritative
(D) Permissive

161. Low expressions of warmth, high critical feedback, and inflexibility on high expectations for maturity and obedience are characteristics of the _____ parenting style.

(A) authoritarian
(B) dismissive
(C) authoritative
(D) permissive

Fill-in-the-Blank Questions

162. In the nature versus nurture debate, family functioning, attachment, and parenting style are _____ influences.

163. The most common approach to measure attachment is the _____ procedure.

164. Infants who are insecurely attached are not _____ by the mother or primary caregiver.

165. Parents who are _____ in meeting the infant's needs promote healthy attachments.

166. Early attachment working models provide a developmental framework for relationships, and interpersonal experiences throughout childhood and adolescence _____ attachment.

167. Diana Baumrind identified four common dimensions of parenting: _____, _____, _____, and _____.

168. Indulging concern for a child's happiness, lack of discipline, low structure, and low expectations for maturity are characteristics of the _____ parenting style.

Short-Answer Questions

169. Explain behaviors that indicate a secure attachment in young children.

170. Describe the Strange Situation procedure.

171. Explain the differences between the three types of attachments.

172. Explain factors that interfere with the child forming a secure attachment.

173. Describe the different behaviors between adult attachment styles.

174. Describe the characteristics of an authoritarian parenting style and the possible outcomes for the child.

175. Describe the characteristics of the authoritative parenting style and the potential outcomes for the child.

CHAPTER 3

Stages of Psychosocial Development

Psychosexual Stages of Development

The psychoanalytic theory originated in the late 1800s with an Austrian physician, Sigmund Freud (1856–1939). Freud first pursued a medical degree and was among the first to conduct neurological research. He earned his medical degree in 1881 and established his practice as a clinical neurologist, but he was also very interested in philosophy and scientific research. However, his career profession was treating patients with psychological disturbances or mental illness. Freud's theory was uniquely different from other schools of psychology at the time because it did not develop out of scientific research, it wasn't taught in the universities, and its focus was on abnormal behaviors.

Freud presented the idea that behaviors are unconsciously driven and are not the results of rational choices. His theories developed out of his clinical practice where he treated patients with hysteria. Freud determined that most of his patients' problems could be linked to earlier childhood experiences, and he believed that sensual satisfaction is associated with childhood needs, challenges, and conflicts. Freud was among the first to emphasize the importance of child development, which he outlined in a five-stage model of psychosexual development.

According to Sigmund Freud, development in the first six years progresses through five stages. At each stage, sexual interest and pleasure are focused on a particular part of the body. For example, the mouth during infancy (the oral stage), the anus during early childhood (the anal stage), and the genitalia later in the preschool years (the phallic stage). Following a period of sexual latency, considered the fourth stage, the adolescent enters into the genital stage, which lasts throughout adulthood.

Freud believed that three primary aspects of personality form over the first five years; id, ego, and superego. The biological self (id) is active at birth, and its purpose is to ensure survival. The id is self-serving and is driven toward pleasure, satisfaction, and gratification. As a child's understanding matures and he or she learns that acting on instinct and self-interest is not always appropriate, the rational self (ego) develops. Behaviors are then driven more by how to get one's needs met in an acceptable way, taking into consideration the consequences of actions and not just what one wants. During preschool years, the child begins to experience guilt when behaviors are disapproved of by the parent. This consideration for obeying the parent comes from the superego, and Freud explained it as an internalized parent, the source of conflict between the pleasure of gratification and the guilt of doing something parent-disapproved. The ego works to satisfy both the wants of the id and the morals of the superego. As a child ages, the conflicts become more complex as experiences and development continue through the five psychosexual developmental stages. Psychosexual development in Freud's stage theory is based on biological instincts and drives and the satisfaction coming from need fulfillment brings sensual gratification.

The oral stage, birth through the first year, is characterized by the infant's energy channeled toward satisfying needs through the mouth. Sucking, crying, and cooing are important behaviors during this time of life. Sucking provides nourishment and comfort; crying regulates temperature and brings awareness to others; and cooing triggers warmth, attention, and affection from others. When mother responds by fulfilling the infant's need, the relationship is positive and nurturing, and the infant learns to accept the parent as contributing to conflict resolution. The ego develops as the parent helps the infant learn how to delay gratification; and, consistency in satisfying needs, according to Freud, leads to a calm personality.

After the first year, the infant enters into the anal stage, which is marked by energies directed toward control over self. Control over the body, in particular the anal area, becomes the source of pleasure. As the anal sphincter develops, the child learns that he or she can control holding and releasing. The second year, is a typical time for parents to begin toilet training, and efforts to control elimination activities begin. The ego continues to grow as the child gains control and then conforms to the expectations of the parent in the process.

Between ages three and five, children are in the phallic stage, characterized by focus primarily on the genital region. Children experience pleasurable sensations from fondling the genitals, and sexual drives are often directed as crushes toward the opposite-sex parent. Freud referred to this phenomenon among male children as the Oedipus complex, and among female children, the Electra complex. According to Freud, children first experience jealousy toward the same-sex parent and may have thoughts about replacing the parent. Sexual gratification at this age is constrained by parent values and disciplinary measures. However, Freud asserts that the ego finds a way to balance the drives of the id and the fears of the superego, and children overcome urges by identifying with the same-sex parent.

After age six, Freud believed children enter into a period of latency in which psychosexual urges are quiet. The id, ego, and superego continue to refine personality, though children are busy adopting roles and learning relevant skills. This period of calm ends with the onset of puberty, and children move into the genital stage, the final stage lasting through adulthood. Late adolescence and adulthood ego works to keep id and superego in balance as freedoms to pursue intimacy increase. Because fulfilling responsible adult roles is important, the young adult can resist sexual impulsive gratifications to engage in work, pursue higher education, and potentially start a family.

Each stage has a potential conflict, and how the child experiences and resolves the conflict, especially during the first three stages, determines personality patterns throughout life. Freud asserted that a crisis can occur at any stage and may lead to a fixation in personality. For example, overindulging in or denial of non-nurturing sucking in infancy can lead to an oral fixation, in which children grow up to have greater needs for oral stimulation. Examples of oral fixations include excessive talking, overeating, and chain smoking. Oral fixation may also include emotional behaviors such as crying easily or overwhelming feelings of helplessness. An anal fixation can result from overcontrolling or overindulgent toilet training practices. Adults with anal fixations may be concerned with being overly clean or excessively messy. They may have a strong need for order, or they may be hopelessly disorganized. How children resolve the difficult emotional turmoil of the phallic stage, and the way parents respond to the child, establishes how he or she will cope with postpubertal sexual needs. Adults with phallic fixations may have strongly internalized prohibitions against sexual behavior or against asserting oneself in intimate relationships. They may also be overly self-centered, vain, or flirtatious. Fixations that emerge in the genital stage tend to be sexual impulses and behaviors. While Freud's theory emphasized the important role of the parent-child relationship, it has been criticized for being too focused on unconscious drives and minimizes the role of individual conscious control. It was considered controversial due to an emphasis on sexual experiences and desires.

Multiple-Choice Questions

176. Sucking, crying, and cooing are examples of behaviors associated with the _____.

    (A) anal stage
    (B) phallic stage
    (C) oral stage
    (D) genital stage

177. According to psychoanalytical theory, when the mother's response to her child is inconsistent, the child can develop a _____ surrounding the needs of the associated stage.

    (A) crisis
    (B) complex
    (C) superego
    (D) fixation

178. Taking turns playing with a new toy is an example of how the
     _____ works to satisfy the wants of the _____ and
     _____.

    (A) ego, id, superego
    (B) id, ego, superego
    (C) superego, id, ego
    (D) id, superego, ego

179. The primary crisis of the _____ stage is for the child to gain control
     while conforming to the expectations of the parent in the process.

    (A) oral
    (B) anal
    (C) phallic
    (D) genital

180. What is the stage when children may experience jealousy toward the same-
     sex parent over relationships with the opposite-sex parent, and may have
     thoughts about replacing the same-sex parent?

    (A) Oral
    (B) Anal
    (C) Phallic
    (D) Genital

181. Psychoanalytical theory considers acting on sexual impulses and promiscu-
     ous sexual behaviors as being fixated at the _____ stage.

    (A) oral
    (B) anal
    (C) phallic
    (D) genital

182. Which is not a noted limitation of the psychosexual theory?

    (A) It places too much emphasis on the parent-child relationship.
    (B) It focuses too much on unconscious drives.
    (C) It prompted the idea that early childhood experiences have lasting
        effects.
    (D) It minimized the role of the individual's conscious control over
        behaviors.

Fill-in-the-Blank Questions

183. Sigmund Freud originated the _____, which provides a framework for development of self and personality.

184. Psychoanalytical theory holds that behaviors are_____ driven and are not the results of rational choices.

185. Freud identified five sensitive periods of development during childhood known as _____.

186. Freud described personality as consisting of three aspects of the self: _____, _____, and _____.

187. Freud suggested that within each stage the child faces a potential _____, which largely determines personality patterns throughout life.

188. In Freud's theory, children have a/an _____ when they experience jealousy toward the same-sex parent and may have thoughts about replacing the parent's role with the opposite-sex parent.

189. According to Freud, how children resolve the difficult emotional turmoil of the _____ stage, and the way parents respond to the child, establishes how he or she will cope with postpubertal sexual needs.

Short-Answer Questions

190. Describe the five stages of development in Freud's psychosexual theory.

191. Explain the parent-child crisis and potential personality traits associated with each of the psychosexual stages.

192. Explain Freud's psychoanalytic theory of personality development over the first five years.

193. What are some of the limitations of Freud's psychoanalytical theory?

194. Explain why Freud believed that latency prepared the adolescent for transitioning into adult roles.

195. Why did Freud consider the toilet training years to be a time for heightened parent-child conflict?

196. What reasoning did Freud have for believing a fixated personality can be linked to parenting in childhood?

Psychosocial Stages of Development

Erik Erikson (1902–1994) was trained in child psychoanalysis under Freud. Erikson built on Freud's first five stages of development; however, he did not share the same perspective about the id being the driving force behind all behaviors. His theory held more emphasis on the psychosocial aspects of behavior. He believed that attitudes and feelings toward the self and others are interconnected and always changing. Through the change, there are turning points in personality development for better or worse, or crisis points. Erikson emphasized each person's relationship to the social environment and the importance of family and cultural influences in determining how well prepared individuals are to meet these crises.

Erikson proposed eight developmental stages in which a particular developmental challenge contributes to identity development. He also believed that the outcome of each stage provided a psychosocial component of personality, or an outcome virtue, of which the direction corresponded with the success of the crisis resolution. Successful resolution and positive outcomes of a stage strengthen positive attitudes in the child's sense of self and about others, which further work to ensure successful resolution of a subsequent stage. Likewise, unresolved crisis, or negative outcomes at any stage, creates negative perceptions and expectations of the child's sense of self and about others. Negative outcomes interfere with the child's ability to work through the crisis of upcoming stages. An ongoing accumulation of negative beliefs about the self and others leads to psychological problems. The first five stages correspond with Freud's age periods, but Erikson added three more to extend into adulthood.

Erickson, like Freud, believed that the caregiver's response to meeting the infant's needs in the first year was important. However, Erikson believed that the child would learn how reliable the world around him or her is based on the caregiver's sensitivity. In the first stage of trust versus mistrust (birth to one year), the caregiver's consistent response to the infant's needs for nourishment, comfort, and affection help foster a sense of trust, and the virtue of hope in the infant. If the caregiver's responses are inconsistent, resentful, and nonaffectionate, a child will experience a mistrust about the reliability of others and therefore have a greater sense of fear.

Between ages one and three, Erikson believed that due to advancing physical and cognitive development and abilities, infants and toddlers strive for a sense of independence. During the second stage of autonomy versus shame and doubt, infants and toddlers undergo efforts to gain control over the body, including elimination. Responsive parents encourage appropriate levels of independence with respect to the child's abilities. Sensitivity in helping children practice skills helps the child gain autonomy for a positive sense of self, and willpower to continue practicing with the hope and expectation of success. However, if parents are overly controlling, insist upon a rigid schedule, and are impatient with the child's efforts to do things on his or her own, the child will experience shame and doubt. Overly critical responses to mistakes the child makes while learning skills and toilet training can lead to a greater self-doubt. Self-doubt can negatively influence a child's attitude about performing future tasks and weaken the child's willpower to stick it out while failing at a task during the learning phase. A child who has successfully resolved a sense of trust and hope in stage 1 will take the time to accomplish a task; however, a child high in fear and mistrust from the first stage may give up after a few tries. Without a good sense of autonomy and willpower, trust in oneself becomes frail, and children will have low expectations for doing things on their own.

Between ages three and six, children have greater muscle coordination and greatly improved cognitive abilities. The third stage, initiative versus guilt, is a time when children are actively learning and are intrinsically motivated to do more things for themselves. Much of children's play, such as playing house, work, building, and so on is a form of experimenting with more responsible roles. How children approach learning and skill development depends on the resolution of the first two crises stages. At this time children explore imagination, take action to achieve goals, and will also start to experience remorse for their actions. Similar to the previous two stages, sensitive responses providing encouragement and careful demonstrations of desired behaviors will increase the child's sense of purpose and confidence. Likewise, children discouraged and shamed in earlier stages may feel overly guilty when they try to do things but make a mistake or a mess. Shame and guilt are self-conscious behaviors shaped by caregiver response. Shame is marked by withdrawal or distraction from the behavior or setting. Guilt behaviors are followed by readiness to correct mistakes or undo actions. Too much guilt will stifle initiative, and too little will prevent a child from establishing boundaries in goal pursuit and fantasy play. It is necessary to develop a balance between individual needs and wants and the needs of the social system to which one belongs.

Successful resolution of stage 3 is important for overcoming the industry versus inferiority crisis of stage 4. Once children enter into school systems, learning becomes a primary task. Between ages 6 and 12, a child's attention is focused on achievement, and self-concept and self-esteem correlate with what one can do, and how well it can be done. Knowledge and application are central to how one feels about oneself. The positive personality virtue is competence, and the negative outcome is a lack of competence. While caregiver response is still impactful, others outside the family are important as well. Social comparison provides a judgment basis of being the best, good, or the worst at a particular task. Peer culture provides a value system for winning and losing and being first or last. Children strive to find a comfortable balance in order to be accepted in social contexts.

Social identity gains importance as children move through adolescence (ages 12 through 18). Adolescents are starting to make decisions about upcoming adult roles and seeking to define themselves, which is the fifth crisis stage, identity versus role confusion. Erikson, along with developmental psychologist James Marcia, recognized four aspects of identity, vocational, gender, religion, and politics, in which adolescents begin to question and define themselves. Identity in any one area may be achieved through foreclosure of parent's values and expectations such as adopting religious practices, gender roles, or assuming a family trade. Many adolescents will enter into an acceptable stage of moratorium to explore roles before adopting them. College, missions, Peace Corps, and internships allow adolescents and young adults the freedom to explore different career areas without a lifelong commitment. Adolescents who cannot define themselves along these areas of identity are thought to be in a state of role diffusion. Role diffusion is more common among younger adolescents; however, if it persists into early adulthood, it may be a sign of unresolved crisis from an earlier stage and can lead to an inability to establish a secure sense of self. Erikson believed that identity development continues into emerging adulthood and that few adolescents foreclose on all four areas of identity. Successful sense of identity provides the virtue of fidelity that supports being able to commit to long-term relationships.

Erikson originally thought the last three stages of development were progressive as a person transitions through adulthood. The sixth stage, intimacy versus isolation emphasizes Erikson's belief that humans are social creatures. Adult identity stems from social affiliations, partnerships, and roles beginning in emerging adulthood. Intimate relationships of all types provide biopsychosocial satisfaction and demand efforts of the individual, often in the form of sacrificing something of the self. Self-understanding achieved in the previous stage ensures that young adults are secure enough about their identity that they can tolerate differences in others to find love in relationships. Lack of fidelity increases self-protective behaviors, which can lead to isolation. The degree of harm from isolation depends on the outcome it provides; however, isolating to avoid negative aspects of social commitments can instill a fear of intimacy. For many, marriage is a primary benchmark in early adulthood followed by having children.

Generativity versus stagnation, stage 7, is characterized by the adult's attention diverted to providing care for the next generation. Raising children is a common way for adults to make a lasting contribution to the future. However, generativity in middle adulthood can be achieved through sharing generational knowledge and culture norms in other types of relationships, work, and the community. Identity is greatly tied to competence and adequacy. Adults who were unable to achieve intimacy successfully are more likely to become self-absorbed rather than achieve the virtue of care for the well-being and success of upcoming generations. Erikson felt that success in achieving generativity prevented disparity in later adulthood. Self-concept during later adult years is associated with cognitive abilities, physical appearance, relationships, health, and life satisfaction.

The eighth stage, integrity versus despair, is a period in which adults must face limitations and overcome prejudices associated with limitations, while still contributing to the well-being of humanity. Over time, with frequent transitions and role changes that occur in adulthood, social losses accumulate. With age, death and loss become a significant part of life, as familiar people pass away and bring about the reality of one's own mortality. Regret and fear of dying are thought to be indications of despair brought on by accumulated conflicts that have not been resolved. While this stage is typical of later adulthood, age is not a determinant factor. Erikson's model emphasized how an individual's self concept developed and changed over the life span. His psychosocial model is influenced in part by his research on family and social interactions among various cultures, and also from his own experiences as an immigrant adapting to new social environments. Cultural influences, though subject to historical context, are relevant and everyone must find integrity in his or her journey.

Freud and Erikson both believed adulthood echoed childhood experiences. Freud emphasized the dark side of human behavior, whereas Erikson highlighted the relevance of social supports and culture. Erikson believed that human development is lifelong, and an individual's personal journey is within historical and cultural contexts, which provide meaning for the purpose of human societies. Crisis not resolved at an earlier stage can be resolved in a later stage. Identity is not fixed upon transitioning from adolescence into adulthood, and circumstances may lead a person to enter into a particular adult stage at any time. Several theories have developed to provide frameworks to understand how self-concept is shaped among aging adults. In addition to reflecting on a life lived, getting involved in communities, social activities, and making changes to improve health status provide ways for older adults to maintain integrity.

Multiple-Choice Questions

197. Erikson's theory of _____ involves a series of eight stages, each of which consists of a crisis that must be resolved for healthy development across the life span.

(A) autonomy
(B) psychosocial development
(C) integrity
(D) identity

198. The caregiver's response to the infant's needs for nourishment, comfort, and affection helps foster a sense of _____ and the virtue of hope in the infant.

(A) autonomy
(B) trust
(C) integrity
(D) identity

199. Stage 2, _____, is characterized by advancing physical and cognitive development and abilities, and infants and toddlers strive for a sense of independence.

(A) autonomy verses shame and doubt
(B) initiative verses guilt
(C) identity verses intimacy
(D) trust verses mistrust

200. Which of the following is a psychosocial stage in which children are eager to do things for themselves but are vulnerable to parental disapproval and may feel overly guilty when they make a mistake or mess?

(A) Autonomy verses shame and doubt
(B) Initiative verses guilt
(C) Identity verses intimacy
(D) Trust verses mistrust

201. College, missions, Peace Corps, and internships allow adolescents and young adults the freedom to explore different career areas without a life-long commitment. These are examples of

(A) identity achieved
(B) moratorium
(C) foreclosure
(D) identity diffusion

202. Self-understanding promotes a secure identity in young adults that allows them to find intimacy and avoid

(A) isolation
(B) guilt
(C) mistrust
(D) generativity

203. Engaging in community outreach, parenting, and mentorship are ways adults fulfill the need for

(A) intimacy
(B) foreclosure
(C) identity
(D) generativity

Fill-in-the-Blank Questions

204. Parents' sensitive responses of encouragement and careful demonstrations of desired behaviors will increase a child's sense of purpose and confidence and help the child avoid excessive _____ over making mistakes.

205. Erikson emphasizes that adult _____ grows out of social affiliations, partnerships, and roles beginning in adolescence and continuing into emerging adulthood.

206. _____ is characterized by an adult's efforts to make a contribution to the future and the next generation.

207. Regret and fear of dying may be indications of _____ brought on by accumulated conflicts that have not been resolved.

208. Children of authoritarian parents are likely to experience _____ shame and doubt than children of authoritative parents.

209. The four areas in which adolescents and young adults pursue identity development are _____, _____, _____, and _____.

210. Peer supports provide a value system for developing _____ and confidence in school-age children and adolescents.

Short-Answer Questions

211. Erikson believed that upon gaining self-awareness, children are motivated toward autonomy. Explain what increases pride or shame in early childhood.

212. In what way does a formal school setting help children build self-concept?

213. Describe the significance of identity on relationships in early adulthood.

214. Compare and contrast Erikson's and Freud's stages of development.

215. Describe in terms of commitment and exploration the four ways in which adolescents and young adults approach identity development.

216. Explain why going to college is an appropriate moratorium in identity development.

217. In what way does resolving the generativity crisis prepare the older adult for resolving the integrity versus despair crisis?

Maslow's Hierarchy of Needs

Abraham Maslow (1908–1970) was a humanistic psychologist who felt that the psychoanalytical perspective placed too much emphasis on problems and negative outcomes. He researched the healthy side of human psychology, focusing his research on the qualities of people who were highly accomplished and exceptional in their life. He organized his findings into a hierarchal model that emphasized positive intentions driven by need fulfillment. The highest level in the model is self-actualization, or a state of complete self-fulfillment and acceptance. Self-actualized individuals tend to maintain an objective perception, have full acceptance of themselves, are committed and dedicated to their work or ambitions, and have a heightened sense of creativity. Arriving at a state of self-actualization is not a destiny but part of the experience of life. Self-actualized people have a need for independence and resist conforming while at the same time have a need for social interest and a desire for the growth of humanity. Maslow declared that self-actualized persons have peak experiences, or moments of profound love, understanding, and happiness in which there is a sense of complete harmony, oneness, or goodness. Although these experiences do not last long, Maslow believed that as people satisfy higher-level needs, peak experiences occur more often.

Maslow found that basic needs, or deficit needs, must be satisfied before moving toward higher-level needs. Basic needs include survival necessities such as nourishment and shelter, and social necessities such as freedom (rights) and opportunities to learn and grow interpersonally. The order of the hierarchy is important because the needs at each level are the motivators. Maslow believed that humans are motivated to grow and develop personally, and as basic needs are met, motivation for personal growth follows. The first level includes physiological needs of food, sleep, and sex. When physiological needs are met, people are motivated to acquire safety and security (level two), such as social order, work, and a sense of stability. The third level is love and belonging, to feel satisfied and safe in a committed relationship. Maslow proposed relationships could be with friends, family, or romantic partners. When people have met physiological, safety, and belonging needs, they become motivated to advance esteem from self and others. Esteem is the first higher level, where the motivation is directed toward increasing a value rather than filling a deficit. Self-sufficiency and competency are key to providing a rich, fulfilled, and effortless sense of esteem. Having achieved esteem, individuals begin to acquire high degrees of acceptance of themselves, others, and events. Maslow also distinguished the self-actualized from others by the way they approach fulfilling needs. Needs can be met through positive or negative behaviors; however, self-actualization and happiness can only be acquired through personal growth and self-understanding.

The hierarchy of needs can be visualized like a ladder progressing from physiological needs (bottom) to self-actualization (top) as Maslow believed few people ever achieve self-actualization, and when they do, it is not a permanent state. Maslow's theory is an effective framework for better understanding of healthy development and adulthood role transition, which was Maslow's ambition. Like the psychoanalytical perspective, he believed that inability to satisfy needs in childhood could interfere with need fulfillment in adulthood. He proposed that individuals could be stuck in one level, unable to move forward because a need could not be satisfied. Maslow believed that to become self-actualized, one must have been secure and confident in childhood, and he emphasized the role of parental acceptance, nurturing, and love during the first two years of life. Developmentally speaking, Maslow's hierarchy of need parallels goals and motivations to achieve common benchmarks of adulthood. He believed that older adults are more likely to be self-actualized than younger adults are, though age is not the specific reason. The model continues to have practical applications in professional settings within and outside of the psychology domain.

Multiple-Choice Questions

218. The highest level in Maslow's hierarchy of needs model is

(A) trust versus mistrust
(B) self-actualization
(C) safety and belonging
(D) socioeconomic status

219. Which of the following does not need to be satisfied before a person can be self-actualized?

(A) Nourishment
(B) Committed relationship
(C) Self-sufficiency
(D) Socioeconomic status

220. Trust and long-term commitment are goals of a person at which level of Maslow's hierarchy?

(A) Food, water, sleep, and sex
(B) Esteem
(C) Safety
(D) Love and belonging

221. What is the theory in psychology that focuses on people's positive potential?

(A) Psychosexual
(B) Humanistic
(C) Cognitive
(D) Social learning

222. Which is a characteristic of an individual seeking to fulfill esteem in Maslow's hierarchy?

(A) Self-sufficient
(B) Peak performance
(C) Self-acceptance
(D) Heightened creativity

223. Tom, a retired architect, has recently taken interest in volunteer work. He experiences an overwhelming feeling of joy and contentment in teaching inner-city kids how to draw buildings and landscapes. Which level(s) is Tom most likely at in Maslow's hierarchy of needs?

(A) Success and esteem
(B) Self-actualization
(C) Love and belonging
(D) Safety

224. Self-actualized individuals differ in _____ from non-self-actualized persons.

(A) wealth
(B) quality
(C) career
(D) age

Fill-in-the-Blank Questions

225. _____ is a state of self-fulfillment in which people realize their highest potential.

226. Abraham Maslow was a _____ psychologist who researched the healthy side of human psychology, focusing his research on the qualities of people who were highly accomplished and exceptional in their life.

227. _____ must be satisfied before higher-levels needs can be pursued.

228. Maslow believed that a parental relationship during the first two years influences the sense of _____ and _____ necessary to achieve self-actualization in adulthood.

229. Feeling a sense of profound love, understanding, happiness, and goodness is a _____ according to Maslow.

230. According to Maslow, _____ adults are more likely to reach self-actualization than _____ adults are.

231. According to Maslow, self-actualization can only be achieved by having had a _____ and _____ childhood.

Short-Answer Questions

232. According to Maslow, what is the five-step hierarchy of basic needs and drives?

233. Explain the importance of the hierarchical organization of Maslow's stage theory.

234. What are some of the primary differences between the psychoanalytical stages of development and Maslow's theory of self-actualization?

235. Mark recently was promoted in his job, and now that he is making a decent salary he is considering buying a house. He has been in a committed relationship with Shelly for over a year and is thinking about asking her to marry him. Explain where Maslow would say Mark is in the hierarchy of needs and self-actualization model.

236. Describe characteristics of a self-actualized individual.

CHAPTER 4

Behavioral Theories and Perspectives

Behaviorism is considered a learning theory because it describes the laws and processes by which behavior is learned. Instead of focusing on stages of development, behaviorism formulated laws of behaviors that operate at every age. Some researchers were curious to know if animal minds were capable of higher human functioning, while others were interested in only the observable behaviors.

Animal Psychology: Stimulus and Response Learning

Animal psychology research provided an objective methodology to studying subjective qualities. Research was done under the assumption that animal minds and human minds functioned similarly as evident by behaviors that resulted from an experience. In other words, animal minds could perform mental tasks similar to humans that included both conscious and unconscious memory. Animal psychology, unlike psychoanalysis, applied an objective methodology to studying subjective qualities. Apparatuses such as puzzle boxes, shuttle boxes, harnesses, and rat mazes were used to demonstrate learning behaviors.

Edward Thorndike (1874–1949) proposed that learning was a series of connections between objectively verifiable situations and responses. He suggested learning happens through trial and error, or instrumental learning. Thorndike experimented with cats and a puzzle box made from a wooden crate with a door that opened by manipulating a lever. Hungry cats were locked inside the box, and a dish of food was placed just outside the door of the box so the cats could see it. Initially the cats pawed through the crate bars, then inside the crate. The first successful pressing of the lever was by accident. Thorndike repeated the experiment, noting any changes in the cats' efforts. In the repeated attempts the cats progressively stopped behaviors that did not result in the door opening. In each attempt, a cat's pawing behaviors remained closer to the latch area until it discovered that only the specific behavior, pressing the lever, was needed. From these experiments, Thorndike developed several laws of learning. The law of effect proposes that actions are associated with situations. Acts that produce satisfaction in a given situation become associated with that situation, and the reinforcement makes it likely the action will recur. The law of exercise proposes that use or disuse influences the strength of associated learning. The more often a behavior or response was used in a given situation, the greater the association. Thorndike's research helped pave the way for behaviorism.

The idea of animal intelligence took off in the early 1900s with the popularity of a horse named Hans. Wilhelm von Osten invested many years in teaching Hans aspects of human intelligence, and it seemed that Hans was able to do math, spelling, and many other human cognitive tasks. Hans was amazingly accurate in each demonstration, leading to the formation of a committee to examine the phenomenon. The committee ruled out any possibility of trickery or fraud and was unable to provide any other explanation besides learning. Soon after, a graduate student assigned to the task applied the experimental method. The student used two groups to ask questions: one that knew the answers, and one that did not know the answers. Hans answered every question correctly for the group aware of the answers, but did not give correct answers for the group that was unaware. He had been unintentionally conditioned to detect cues from the person asking the questions. Osten, by rewarding Hans for correctly responding to these cues, indirectly provided the reinforcement necessary to strengthen the behaviors. Behavioral psychologists continue to explore the role of reinforcement in learning.

Not all animal researchers discounted mental aspects of behaviors. Many exclaimed animals were capable of mental tasks similar to humans, including conscious and unconscious memory. Margaret Floy Washburn (1871–1939) was instrumental in establishing evidence that mental tasks could be observed through behaviors that resulted from an experience. These ideas were widely accepted because of the difficulty in applying the scientific method to unconscious motives and drives highlighted within the psychoanalytic theories. Animal research progressed into the science of behavioral psychology and continues to be an important element in advancing human research. Millions of animals are used for human research annually, and research must be approved through an ethics organization.

John Watson (1878–1958) was among the first to insist that psychology needed to focus on objective and measurable behaviors in order to be taken seriously as a science. While he made contributions to animal psychology, he was criticized for his methods and eventually left that area of research. Watson founded behavioral psychology because he wanted to bring psychology beyond the psychoanalytic perspective. He wanted psychology to focus on what people do, not what they experience. Watson's behaviorism theory relied on experimental measures of observation, observable verbal reports, testing, and conditioned reflex responses. His research attempted to explain instinct, emotion, and thoughts using objective stimulus-response terms.

Instincts, according to Watson, were socially conditioned responses. Watson asserted that children were not born with particular behaviors, but instead the behaviors resulted from early childhood training. According to Watson, any undesirable traits or special talents displayed in childhood could be overridden through learning. He proposed that parenting has everything to do with how adaptive a child is or becomes. He was so confident in the role of a nurturing environment that he claimed he could train any healthy child to become a particular type of person, regardless of the child's talents, abilities, or ancestry.

Watson believed that emotions were physiological responses to specific stimuli. The internal physical reactions are accompanied by a learned overt response that is physically observable. He proposed that emotions could be conditioned to stimuli that otherwise would not be able to elicit them. In his classic experiment, he demonstrated how an infant, Albert, could be conditioned to fear objects such as a rat, a rabbit, and a bunny mask. Albert initially exhibited no prior fears of these objects.

Before age eight months, an infant's fear response is typically specific to loud noises. Watson and colleagues conducted research examining these fear reflexes. In order to demonstrate that emotional reactions are conditioned, they associated an unrelated stimulus, a white rat, with a loud clanking noise. Prior to the experiment, the white rat was a neutral stimulus to the infant. The loud noise was an unconditioned stimulus (US) naturally triggering fear, an unconditioned response (UR). During the experiment, the neutral stimulus was paired with the US, which created the association and led to a conditioned emotional response (CER). After several pairings, Albert began to exhibit fear when presented with the white rat without the loud noise. The white rat had now become a conditioned stimulus (CS), and his fear of it was a conditioned response (CR). In further experiments, Albert seemed to generalize his fear of the white rat to other similar objects, including the rabbit and mask that he was previously unafraid of.

Watson advanced psychology into the scientific realm by founding behaviorism and defining methods for research. His behaviorist philosophy was welcomed, and he was successful in creating a framework for psychology's application beyond the academic and counseling setting.

Multiple-Choice Questions

237. Which of the following was not a major contributor within the behaviorist perspective of psychology?

(A) John Watson
(B) John Locke
(C) B. F. Skinner
(D) Edward Thorndike

238. Edward Thorndike believed that learning was a series of connections between situations and responses. Which is a Thorndike law of learning?

(A) Law of effect
(B) Law of observation
(C) Law of attraction
(D) Law of reinforcement

239. Which apparatus was used by Thorndike to explore trial-and-error learning behaviors in cats?

(A) Skinner box
(B) Puzzle box
(C) Thorndike box
(D) Learning box

240. The _____ states that use or disuse influences the strength of associated learning.

(A) law of exercise
(B) law of effect
(C) law of reinforcement
(D) law of punishment

241. Margaret Floy Washburn (1871–1939) was instrumental in establishing evidence that mental tasks could be observed in an animal's actions. In other words, _____ is evident by the behaviors that resulted directly from an experience.

(A) nativism
(B) predisposition
(C) cognition
(D) motivation

242. Millions of animals are used for human research annually, and research must be approved through a/an _____ organization.

(A) funding
(B) ethics
(C) zoology
(D) behavioral

243. Which of the following is not associated with Watson's behaviorist perspective?

(A) Instincts are socially conditioned responses.
(B) Behaviors are not innate but result from early childhood training.
(C) Undesirable traits can be overridden through learning.
(D) Emotions are not learned responses.

Fill-in-the-Blank Questions

244. Behaviorism is a/an _____ because it describes the laws and processes by which behavior is learned.

245. Behaviorism theories began with _____ subjects in experimental studies.

246. Animal psychology applied a/an _____, using apparatuses such as puzzle boxes, shuttle boxes, harnesses, and rat mazes, to study subjective qualities of learning.

247. Thorndike was interested in _____, or behavior that required an organism to manipulate elements of its environment.

248. The case of Hans, a famous horse that impressed researchers by being able to do math, spelling, and many other human cognitive tasks, demonstrated _____.

249. John Watson asserted that psychology needed to focus on _____ behaviors to be taken seriously as a science.

250. Watson's classic experiment with an infant named Albert demonstrated that the fear reflex can be conditioned and therefore fear is a/an _____.

Short-Answer Questions

251. Explain instrumental learning in Thorndike's experiment with cats in the puzzle box.

252. What is the law of effect? Provide an example.

253. Describe what Thorndike meant by learned associations.

254. Explain what influences the strength of learned associations.

255. Behavioral psychology emphasized experimental research. What was the role of experimental research in understanding Hans, the smart horse?

256. Why did Watson want psychology to focus on predicting and controlling behaviors instead of the unconscious mental processes?

257. Explain what was learned from Watson's classic experiment with an infant, Albert.

Classical Conditioning

Ivan Pavlov (1849–1936), a Russian physiologist, made his contribution to psychology accidently while conducting research on the digestive systems in dogs. In Pavlov's experiment, the apparatus was connected to the dog's saliva glands, and the collected saliva was measured as food was presented. While measuring the salivating behaviors, Pavlov noticed that the dogs began to salivate before the food was presented. He determined that the dogs had learned cues leading to the food presentation. Pavlov declared that animals and humans had respondent reflexes. Respondent conditioning occurs when a particular response becomes linked to a particular stimulus. Pavlov found that the dogs learned to associate food with various neutral stimuli such as a lab coat and the presence of the researcher. Pavlov conducted several experiments exploring the conditioning phenomenon. He began to use different types of stimuli, such as tones and bells, which he always paired with arrival of the dogs' food. The dogs' association of sensory stimuli developed because it was reinforced by the presentation of food that always followed. The tone and other cues became a conditioned stimulus, and the salivating behavior became a conditioned response. Pavlov termed this conditioning process the acquisition phase.

Curious about the strength of associations, Pavlov began exploring how long it would take for the association to go away if the dogs did not receive food. He found that the acquisition behaviors quickly diminished and steadily decreased until the dogs no longer salivated upon hearing the tone. Learning is considered a marked change in behavior; therefore, Pavlov wondered if the extinction process was permanent. Having tracked the trial details during the acquisition phase, Pavlov began a new acquisition phase, which he called the recovery phase. After a period of rest after extinction, usually 24 hours without hearing the tone, Pavlov presented the tone. The dog initially anticipated food, however, without the reinforcement, the dog quickly gave up the expectation. When the recovery phase was repeated, the same results followed. Pavlov concluded that acquisition behaviors may be permanent, but they will not be maintained without reinforcement. Furthermore, after a period of extinction, the behavior can be recovered, however in the absence of reinforcement, the behavior diminishes quickly. Therefore, conditioned learning is permanent, but the reliability of conditioned responses depends on the presence of reinforcement. Classical conditioning is one of the primary learning processes underlying Watson's behaviorism perspective.

In a practical sense, classical conditioning happens every time two unrelated events become connected. People are more likely to experience a state of stress or anxiety when seeing a police car if they have previously been pulled over and given a ticket. Conditioning is stronger for any stimulus that creates an emotional effect, such as fear, gratification, or happiness. Lunch bells, the smell of cookies baking, and alarm clocks are common examples of stimuli that have conditioned human physiologic responses.

Multiple-Choice Questions

258. _____ is a marked and relatively permanent change in behaviors as a result of experience.

(A) Reinforcement
(B) Learning
(C) Motivation
(D) Extinction

259. Pavlov's experiments with dogs that salivated when they heard a specific noise provide an example of _____.

(A) classical conditioning
(B) observational learning
(C) operant conditioning
(D) reinforcement

260. A/an _____ is a stimulus that does not naturally bring about the desired response.

(A) conditioned stimulus
(B) unconditioned stimulus
(C) neutral stimulus
(D) acquisitioned stimulus

261. In Pavlov's experiment, salivating to the tone was the _____?

(A) conditioned stimulus
(B) unconditioned response
(C) conditioned response
(D) unconditioned stimulus

262. Conditioned responses are permanent as long as the pairing is _____.

(A) repeated
(B) frequent
(C) reinforced
(D) pleasurable

263. In _____, conditioning is stronger for any stimulus that creates an emotional effect, such as fear, gratification, or happiness.

(A) classical conditioning
(B) observational learning
(C) operant conditioning
(D) reinforcement

264. Lisa calls her cat into the house at night by shaking his cat food box. In terms of classical conditioning, the cat food box is a _____.
    (A) conditioned stimulus
    (B) unconditioned response
    (C) conditioned response
    (D) unconditioned stimulus

Fill-in-the-Blank Questions

265. _____, a Russian psychologist, made a major contribution to psychology while studying digestive systems in dogs.

266. Pavlov termed respondent conditioning of reflexes as classical conditioning, stating this type of learning happens every time two unrelated events become _____.

267. Classical conditioning is one of the primary learning processes of the _____ perspective.

268. The dog's association of sensory stimuli developed because it was _____ by the presentation of food that always followed.

269. In the _____ phase, the reinforcement is removed from the conditioned stimulus.

270. Eric loves to tickle his little brother. Before he tickles his brother, he holds his fingers up and wiggles them, telling his brother, "Here come the ticklers." Now all he has to do is hold up his fingers, and his brother starts to laugh. This is an example of _____.

271. In the scenario in Question 270, holding the fingers up is the _____.

272. In the scenario in Question 270, the laughing response to the wiggling fingers is a/an _____.

Short-Answer Questions

273. What theory did Pavlov provide to explain the dogs' salivating behavior during his digestive research?

274. List and describe the four elements of classical conditioning.

275. Explain the acquisition phase of classical conditioning.

276. Describe the extinction process of an acquired behavior.

277. The last two times Mindy was left at day care, another child hit her and made her cry. Today when her mother takes her to day care, Mindy begins to cry when they walk in the door. The child hitting Mindy was a/an _____ that brought about a/an _____, her cry.

278. Mindy's mother is upset because the day care has become the _____ for Mindy's crying.

279. In the above scenario, Mindy's crying at the sight of the day care facility is a/an _____ .

280. What would have to happen in order for Mindy's associated learning to become extinct?

Operant Conditioning

Watson and Pavlov established evidence that behavior is a response to a stimulus cue, and the behavior is shaped or controlled by a stimulus outcome. Other researchers such as Edward Tolman and B. F. Skinner continued experiments on behavior, learning, and conditioning.

Purposive Behavior: Edward Tolman (1886–1959)

Tolman believed that a purpose drives behavior. He reintroduced the concept of mental activity or consciousness. Tolman held his perspective to the strict behaviorist methodology and discounted the organism's experience or introspection on the event. In Tolman's perspective, purposive behaviors were objectively defined as goals and behaviors that serve as means to an end. Changes in behaviors served as objective measures of learning. Tolman proposed that behaviors are triggered by many factors including environmental stimuli, physiological drives, heredity, previous training, and age. These intervening variables are capable of triggering observable behaviors, which lead to outcomes. The outcomes of behaviors do more than satisfy needs and drives; they work to establish a relationship between the organism and its environment. A combination of cues and expectations affect future performances. Tolman and others at the time were pursuing a mechanistic perspective to learning, the role of reinforcement, and the lack of importance of conscious experience. Behaviorists accepted that reinforcement was central and proposed that when the reinforcement reduced a biological need, the behavior became stronger.

Operant Conditioning: B. F. Skinner (1904–1990)

Skinner found meaning in both Watson's and Pavlov's research, and he believed that the outcomes of learning are more influenced by the organism's enjoyment rather than simply repeated exposure. Skinner believed in instrumental conditioning, or a learning process in which a particular action is followed by something either desired or unwanted. Positive outcomes increase the likelihood that a person or animal will repeat the action, whereas something unwanted makes the action less likely to be repeated. Because Skinner's theory is an early behaviorist framework, very little attention is given to the inner workings of thoughts or feelings in regard to shaping the behaviors. An emphasis is placed on the environmental cues and outcomes.

An underlying belief in Skinner's theory of operant conditioning is that behaviors are largely due to genetic endowment and environmental reinforcements, which can be a reward or punishment. Pleasant or pain-relieving outcomes are reward reinforcements because they are more likely to reproduce the actions that led to the outcome, whereas unpleasant outcomes are punishments and will lead to a decrease or elimination of those actions in order to prevent a repeat of the undesired outcome. Reinforcements increase the likelihood of a behavior occurring; punishments decrease the likelihood of a behavior occurring. Skinner introduced the idea that reinforcements and punishments could be both positive and negative. Importantly, positive and negative do not imply pleasant or unpleasant, but instead the addition or removal of a stimulus. When a stimulus is given to increase a behavior, it is a positive reinforcement; however, if something is removed to increase a behavior, it is a negative reinforcement. The same is true for punishments, except the goal is to decrease a behavior. Additionally, reinforcers can be classified as primary (occurring naturally) or conditioned by learned association to a primary reinforcer.

In Skinner's experiments, animals, usually rats or pigeons, performed some action and a response occurred. When the response was pleasurable, the animal would repeat the action; but if it was painful, the animal would not repeat the action. Skinner developed an apparatus box containing a lever that when pressed or pecked would release a food pellet or a seed. He also experimented with conditioned learning by adding visual and auditory stimuli paired with the pressing or pecking behaviors leading to the dispensing reinforcement (food). Once the behavior was consistent, Skinner began wondering about the stability of reinforced behaviors. The next step was to examine changes in learning responses when rewards were delivered under varying schedules.

Skinner found that behaviors were stronger when reinforcements were delivered in continuous short and achievable schedules. The schedule could be by ratio or interval, fixed or variable, but if the schedule was too hard or too long, the behaviors would weaken. Ratio schedules dispense reinforcement after so many behavior occurrences, while interval schedules are set amounts of time. A fixed schedule implies that a set number of occurrences, or a set amount of time, must precede dispensing of the reinforcement. Variable schedules have no set amount of time, or number of occurrences, and are unpredictable in dispensing reinforcement. Ratio schedules tend to produce higher rates of response than intervals. Variable interval schedules are more reliable than fixed intervals in maintaining desired response behaviors.

Skinner also found that the frequency of reinforcement also affects the extinction of a response. Behaviors reinforced by intermittent rewards take much longer to extinguish than those reinforced continuously because intermittent reward expectations are not based on a continuous reinforcement. The organism learns that persistence pays off and will persist in the behavior under the belief that sooner or later it will pay off.

These concepts are central to behavior modification in establishing a desired behavior or in modifying an existing one. Complex behaviors are modified by reinforcement schedules that shape behaviors based on successive approximations. Rewarding behaviors that are part of the approach to completing the desired behavior is necessary for complex behaviors, to keep organisms motivated in the learning process.

Multiple-Choice Questions

281. Tolman believed that a/an _____ drives behavior, and _____ behaviors were objectively defined as goals in which behaviors serve as means to an end.

(A) ambition, ambitious
(B) determination determined
(C) instinct, instinctive
(D) purpose, purposive

282. Reinforcements can be

(A) both positive and negative
(B) only positive
(C) only negative
(D) neither positive nor negative

283. Learning in which the outcomes of one's behavior determines the likelihood of the behavior being repeated is called

(A) operant condition
(B) classical conditioning
(C) behavior modification
(D) intermittent reinforcement

284. Taking away a teenager's cell phone until homework is completed is using a

(A) positive punishment
(B) negative reinforcement
(C) positive reinforcement
(D) negative punishment

285. Providing an incentive in order to increase a behavior is using a

(A) positive punishment
(B) negative reinforcement
(C) positive reinforcement
(D) negative punishment

286. In operant conditioning, punishment

(A) increases the desired behavior
(B) decreases the undesired behavior
(C) decreases the desired behavior
(D) increases the undesired behavior

287. Conditioning involves _____behaviors, whereas operant conditioning involves _____ behaviors.

(A) abnormal, modified
(B) established, new
(C) involuntary, voluntary
(D) rewards, punishment

Fill-in-the-Blank Questions

288. When pigeons peck on a lighted lever in order to receive a pellet, the pecking is considered a/an _____ behavior.

289. Tolman proposed that behaviors are _____ by many factors including environmental stimuli, physiological drives, heredity, previous training, and age.

290. To the behaviorists, the outcomes of behavior (reinforcement) influence the strength of learning, and when the reinforcement _____, the behavior becomes stronger.

291. Tolman emphasized the role of _____ thought, while Skinner emphasized the role of environmental cues and _____.

292. Skinner asserted that outcomes of learning are influenced more by the _____ rather than simply repeated exposure.

293. _____ is the process of establishing a desired behavior or modifying an existing one.

294. Skinner found that behaviors were stronger when reinforcements were delivered in _____ and achievable schedules.

Short-Answer Questions

295. Describe the difference between operant conditioning and classical conditioning.

296. What is the role of reinforcements in Skinner's theory of operant conditioning?

297. Explain the effect of delivering rewards under varying schedules on learning responses.

298. Describe Skinner's operant conditioning experiments with pigeons using reinforcement.

299. Why do behaviors reinforced by intermittent rewards take much longer to extinguish than those reinforced continuously?

300. Describe the most effective approach to shaping complex behaviors.

301. David and Kim have been recommended by their doctor to lose 15 pounds and to improve their cholesterol levels. Both have normal blood pressure, though David's is approaching high. The doctor approved their starting an exercise program with no restrictions and suggested a diet modification plan as well. Discuss a behavior modification plan for David and Kim that utilizes positive and negative reinforcements and punishments, and a schedule for rewards.

Social Behavior and Learning

Social behaviorism was in many ways part of a transitional movement toward cognitive psychology. Psychologists such as Julian Rotter (1916–2014) and Albert Bandura (b. 1925) proposed a social component to learning, stating that the outcome expectations are influenced by others as well as the social context.

Rotter was critical of the original behaviorist discounting of cognitive processes. He placed more emphasis on perceptions and beliefs about personal control over reinforcement outcomes. He believed that people tend to have a dominant internal or external locus of control. People with an internal locus of control believe they have a great deal of influence on outcomes, while those with an external locus of control believe outcomes are beyond their influence.

The principles of Rotter's social learning theory are based on the idea that people form subjective expectations about the reinforcements that follow their behaviors. People also formulate the likelihood that particular behaviors will produce specific reinforcements, and they can modify those behaviors to ensure the desired reinforcement. Last, the value of reinforcement is determined by the individual, and it can be situation specific. People live in psychological environments; therefore, the value of a reinforcement differs between individuals and can change in different situations. Rotter discovered that successful outcomes do not change an individual's belief about perceived control.

Rotter believed locus of control demonstrated achievement motivation and the tendency to conform to others, which was reflected by an internal or external pattern of perceiving control. He developed a scale to measure internal and external locus of control, and locus of control remains a valid measure in research.

Bandura proposed that learning is a reciprocal process between the individual and the environment, and that the interactions of humans in their environment were most important. As a behaviorist, he acknowledged that the environment cues an action or response by an individual, and that rewards or reinforcements were important in acquiring or modifying behaviors. However, unlike the extreme behaviorist perspective, he believed the response is not an automatic, instinctive drive, but is instead the result of internalized thoughts and emotional interactions. In other words, the individual is consciously aware of the response, anticipates the outcome, and has expectations of the outcome on a future occurrence of the response.

Bandura's theory began as social learning theory incorporating the behaviorist learning perspective with the inclusion of a social-cognitive element. Bandura added that humans learn vicariously, and behaviors can be reinforced by observing the outcomes of others' actions. He proposed that the social environment influenced learning by modeling behaviors and reinforcing outcomes. Research on mirror neurons demonstrates that observing another perform a task triggers the same neurons to fire as if the observer were actually performing the task. For example, mirror neurons make it possible for an inexperienced person such as a child or a new employee to quickly learn new tasks by watching and imitating others performing the task. However, social learning further suggests that learning is dependent upon more than observing and imitating, to include the individual's cognitive efforts in processing observed outcomes. It holds that people are more likely to learn new behaviors by observing and imitating, or modeling, the behavior of other people they consider admirable, powerful, nurturing, or similar. In addition, the individual gains significant information about the consequences of behaviors. When the behaviors of others result in favorable consequences, there is greater likelihood that the observer will repeat those behaviors. Likewise, punishment, rejection, and other negative outcomes that follow another's behaviors decrease the likelihood of observers adopting those behaviors.

Researchers have explored the effect of observed violence on childhood behaviors and found that once the behavior has been modeled, it becomes part of the child's problem-solving schema. In his classic experiment, Bandura and colleagues used Bobo dolls to demonstrate this phenomenon. Children who witnessed a model perform aggressive acts on the Bobo doll exhibited imitated aggression as well as significantly more ways (than observed in the model) to be aggressive.

Social learning is related to perceptions, interpretations, self-understanding, social reflection, and self-efficacy. Bandura believed that an individual's beliefs and self-understanding directly influence that person's life. He placed a great deal of emphasis on self-efficacy, holding that it demonstrates a sense of competence for dealing with problems in life. Higher degrees of self-efficacy are consistently found to associate with greater levels of success, whereas lower degrees are associated with hopelessness and poorer psychological health. These are human elements that behaviorists purposely discounted and took great steps to keep out of psychology research. Bandura argued against extreme behaviorists' denial that humans interact with each other in their environment and held that psychological research should not overlook that interaction.

Bandura's theory is currently referred to as a social cognitive theory having a strong emphasis on how an individual's actions are shaped by the social environment as well as the meanings and importance assigned by the individual. His behavioral therapy approach is practiced in clinical, business, and education settings. Self-efficacy continues to be a popular measure in health and social science research.

Multiple-Choice Questions

302. Social behaviorists emphasize that outcome _____ shape behaviors and that behaviors are influenced by others and the social context.

(A) expectations
(B) consequences
(C) reinforcements
(D) punishments

303. Rotter believed that all of the following except _____ are represented in one's patterns of internal and external locus of control.

(A) perceptions
(B) involuntary responses
(C) beliefs
(D) outcome expectations

304. Bandura's social learning theory is unlike the traditional behaviorist stimulus and response learning theory because it emphasized _____ learning.

(A) voluntary
(B) instrumental
(C) observational
(D) involuntary

305. Jason watches his older brother smoking outside with his friends. According to Bandura, Jason will likely

(A) learn to smoke too
(B) learn that smoking is not healthy
(C) not smoke
(D) tell his brother not to smoke

306. _____ is an assimilation of perceptions, interpretations, self-understanding, social reflection, and self-efficacy.

(A) Operant learning
(B) Classical learning
(C) Instrumental learning
(D) Social learning

307. Within the social learning perspective, _____ is to Bandura as _____ is to Rotter.

(A) self-esteem, self-efficacy
(B) self-efficacy, locus of control
(C) locus of control, self-esteem
(D) locus of control, self-efficacy

308. _____ is concerned with the perceived relationship individuals have with their environment and the effect they can have on outcomes.

(A) Self-efficacy
(B) Locus of control
(C) Self-esteem
(D) Social identity

Fill-in-the-Blank Questions

309. _____ locus of control represents a high level of perceived self-control over an outcome, whereas _____ locus of control suggests belief that an outcome is beyond an individual's control.

310. Both of Terry's parents have type 2 diabetes, and he believes that he will eventually get it despite any efforts to eat right or exercise regularly. Terry is high on _____ locus of control for diabetes onset.

311. Albert Bandura believed that behavior responses are the result of _____ thought and _____ interactions.

312. Bandura believed that learning can take place by observing the _____ of others' behaviors.

313. Sherry and Cindy walk together at the park twice a week. Lately Sherry has noticed how fit Cindy seems to be. Cindy tells her she is swimming and doing yoga three days a week. It dawns on Sherry that she could do those things, and she makes plans to go with Cindy. Sherry most likely has _____ for the physical activities and a/an _____ locus of control for keeping fit.

314. Studies on aggression in children show that once a child observes an act of violence, _____.

315. Higher degrees of _____ are consistently found to associate with greater levels of success, whereas lower degrees are associated with hopelessness and poorer psychological health.

Short-Answer Questions

316. In what way did Bandura agree with the behaviorist perspective, and in what way did he disagree?

317. Explain why the evaluation of the outcome or consequences of another's behavior is what shapes behaviors.

318. Explain the influence of watching violent media in increased aggression in children according to social learning theory.

319. What is the difference between self-efficacy and locus of control in effecting behavior?

320. Explain how changing self-efficacy can create change in a target behavior of increasing exercise in an older adult.

CHAPTER 5

Cognitive Theories and Perspectives

Information Processing Theory

Cognitive psychology was formally recognized during the mid-twentieth century. Forerunners to the foundation of cognitive psychology include George Miller (1945–2012), noted for being among the first to assert similarities between human minds and computer processes, and Ulric Neisser (1928–2012), recognized as the "father" of cognitive psychology. Both Miller and Neisser aspired to look beyond the dominant behaviorist perspective.

Miller is well known for contributions in understanding memory spans, noting that many people were able to recall seven pieces of information accurately, and most were able to within plus or minus two. Miller called his research the "magic number seven." Miller explained differences between abilities were due to the type of information memorized. For example, seven was accurate when it came to single or chunks of digits, but when it came to words, four was more accurate.

Neisser practiced under Maslow, and although his research formally introduced the cognitive perspective, he intended his research to be integrated with psychology as a whole. Neisser's research extended many structuralism ideas, and in particular he highlighted the critical role of the sensory system in all cognitive processes (memory, sensation, perception, problem solving, and so on). Neisser's ambitions were to bring psychology into a practical realm and not be solely reliant upon laboratory studies.

The formal cognitive school of thought focuses on the processes involved in acquiring knowledge, and how the mind organizes experiences and processes sensory information. Cognitive psychologists focus on how the human mind manipulates information. The computer metaphor provided a popular working model for explaining how information is stored in memory, the processes of recalling stored information, and how new information could be integrated with previously stored information to form new knowledge. The information processing theory, as it became known, asserts that human thinking processes are like computer processes. The mind receives sensory input comparable to data input, working memory processes information much like data analysis, and information is stored as memory with markers and held until recalled similarly to data output. The stored information can be retrieved by more than one path, however, and unlike computers, human cognition requires brain maturation, selective attention, and automatization before it can be efficient.

Humans have highly effective sensory receptors that receive external information and send it along neural axons within the central nervous system. These impulses travel to the brain and become sensory memory, most of which lasts for less than one second before it decays. Obviously, this is good, considering the enormous amount of sensory information we encounter on a daily basis. You might relate this to as a basic browser web page. There are many pieces of information on a typical web page; however, most of the time we ignore more than half of it. In other words, you use selective attention because your focus is on something specific. However, if in the brief moment between opening the page and executing the intended task, something catches your attention, you may decide it is important enough to look into. Attending to initial sensory input moves the information into working memory for further analysis.

Information that makes it to working memory is still within the neural system; it is not stored information, and it can last between 10 and 15 seconds before starting to decay. Rehearsing this information, such as when we repeat new phone numbers, can slow down decay for a brief time—usually for only another 10 to 15 seconds. Working memory also has a limited capacity, and it cannot multitask well, which is why many people struggle to recall what they were reading after an interruption. The ability to understand memory in order to use it, or metamemory, is necessary to move information from working memory to long-term memory storage. Metamemory involves strategic manipulation and organization of information such as rehearsal, activation, pattern matching, and response generation.

Storing information for a long time involves the hippocampal region of the brain. The hippocampus plays an essential role in the initial storage of information, working much like a directory board. By frequently visiting the directory board, we become familiar with how to locate the information we need. After a while, we do not need to go to the directory board because we know how to access the desired information without it. The hippocampus is most essential for storing information. If it is damaged, new memories cannot be stored; however, old ones can still be retrieved. Automatization, or to automatically utilize stored information, involves other areas of the brain. For example, think of all the tasks involved in driving a car, and how little conscious thought you put into performing them. Using reliable memory storage strategies, such as rehearsal, facilitates tasks becoming routine and makes it easier to recall important information later.

In addition to receiving sensory stimuli and sending them to the working memory, the sensory system is also involved in storing information into long-term memory. Therefore, the sensory system is important in the retrieval process, working as a cue to assist in bringing the information to mind again. A retrieval cue is something associated with the stored information, such as a smell, sound, or visual image. Accessing stored knowledge information requires becoming aware of how the information was stored. Cues can serve as reminders of how the information was encoded for memory and thereby make it accessible later. For example, taking notes using concept mapping can provide a visual map of key concepts and relationships between them. Remembering the visual image of the map can trigger the memory of the other related information. Memorized information is more easily retrieved when sensory conditions are similar to when the information was stored.

Brain maturation is essential for ongoing advancing cognitive processes, including metamemory and metacognition. Myelin is a fatty coating on the axons that speeds signals between neurons. Extensive myelination results in faster communication pathways necessary for efficient information processing. Quicker information processing makes selective attention and quicker reaction times possible, promoting efficient storing of information to memory. Metamemory, the understanding of how memory works, is necessary to be able to apply effective strategies for storing and retrieving information such as preparing for exams. These abilities also advance reasoning and logical thinking, which make metacognition possible. Metacognition is the ability to assess a cognitive task in order to determine the best way to accomplish it. Metamemory and metacognition are first apparent in school-age children but continue to improve with age. The efficiency of both processes is dependent upon the myelin sheath, and if this sheath begins to break down, reaction times and accuracy of the information communicated along the neuron become vulnerable. Common causes of myelin breakdown are illness, malnutrition, and aging.

Multiple-Choice Questions

321. _____ was noted for being among the first to assert similarities between human minds and computer processes.

    (A) Ulric Neisser
    (B) Jean Piaget
    (C) George Miller
    (D) Abraham Maslow

322. _____ psychologists focus on how the human mind manipulates information.

    (A) Behavioral
    (B) Social learning
    (C) Psychoanalytical
    (D) Cognitive

323. The information processing theory was inspired by the knowledge of how _____ function.

    (A) animals' brains
    (B) upper-class businessmen
    (C) computers
    (D) medical professionals

324. Information in the sensory memory lasts for less than _____ before it decays.

(A) 3 seconds
(B) 7 seconds
(C) 1 second
(D) 15 seconds

325. The ability to automatically utilize stored information, _____, involves other areas of the brain.

(A) working memory
(B) sensory memory
(C) long-term memory
(D) automatization

326. Information in the working memory can last for up to _____ before it decays.

(A) 3 seconds
(B) 7 seconds
(C) 1 second
(D) 15 seconds

327. Attending to initial sensory input moves the information into _____ memory for further analysis.

(A) working
(B) sensory
(C) long-term
(D) automatization

Fill-in-the-Blank Questions

328. _____focuses on the processes involved in acquiring knowledge, and how the mind organizes experiences and processes sensory information.

329. _____ involves strategic manipulation and organization of information such as rehearsal, activation, pattern-matching, and response generation.

330. The human brain differs from a computer in that it requires _____, _____, and _____.

331. The _____ plays an essential role in the initial storage of information.

332. Working memory also has a _____ capacity, and information must be _____ to make it to long-term memory.

333. _____of neurons results in faster communication pathways necessary for efficient information processing.

334. _____ is the ability to assess a cognitive task in order to determine the best way to accomplish it.

Short-Answer Questions

335. From Miller's perspective on memory recall, explain the best way to remember a long list of information.

336. Based on the information processing theory, in what ways is the human mind similar to a computer, and it what ways is it different?

337. Explain the three types of memory and how we form a memory for later recall.

338. Explain why the computer metaphor provided a popular model for understanding cognition.

339. Explain how the hippocampus works like an information index system such as a directory board or a recipe card.

340. What is the importance of metacognition in making behavior changes?

341. Explain the importance of myelination in cognitive development.

Stages of Cognitive Development

Piaget's Periods of Cognitive Development

Cognitive theorist Jean Piaget (1896–1980) spent a great deal of time with children, listening to the ways in which they explained novel experience. Piaget was one of the first to assert that people construct knowledge. He explains human intellect as mental representations of the world and how it works based on our experiences in it. Piaget proposed four periods in which cognitive maturity advances according to the way people acquire new knowledge and how knowledge advances. These periods are sensorimotor (six stages from birth to 2 years), preoperational (ages 2 to 6), concrete operational (ages 7 to 11), and formal operational (age 12 to adulthood).

Sensorimotor Intelligence

At birth, sensory systems are fully active but not equally developed. According to Piaget, continued brain maturation depends on sensorimotor stimulation and reflexes. Sensation (sensory input), perception (analysis/meaning), and motor movement create a sensorimotor neural system. In this system are rapidly expanding pathways that allow infants to make adaptations to reflexive behaviors and form habits such as thumb sucking, gross motor skills such as walking, fine motor activities such as tying one's shoes, and advance in cognitive activities such as planning actions based on expected outcomes. While the sensorimotor system is the vehicle of learning for the infant, new experiences are transformed into knowledge through two methods: assimilation, adding new schemas into existing knowledge, and accommodation, modifying existing schemas to form new ones.

An infant's first learning experiences take place through reflexes, or behaviors present at birth, including the processes of sucking, tasting, and biting. Until babies can grasp and navigate objects to their mouth independently, everything put into their mouth is a source of food or comfort. As a result, among the first assimilated knowledge is that we feel better when we put something in our mouth, and everything that goes into the mouth will provide food or comfort. With improved motor skill come new abilities and experiences. Once an infant is capable of grasping, for example a rattle, and bringing an object to his or her mouth, the sounds, texture, and hardness or softness of the object provides a new experience. Newly accommodated knowledge develops for things put in the mouth that are not edible or comfortable. Throughout the first few months, visual acuity reaches its full potential, moving from blurred images and black and white to colored and more focused images. Around eight months, infants are capable of object permanence, the idea that something can exist even when it is out of sight. Piaget believed that the infant's participation, emotional expression, and focused attention in sensorimotor activities are indicative of early signs of purposeful intention, or goal-directed behaviors in which the infant actively tries to make events happen. Infants continue to adapt new knowledge and anticipate that activities will happen. For example, infants quickly assimilate parent response to the sounds they make and anticipate that the parent will respond accordingly to the sound. As the child's brain matures, acquired information increases and assimilation and accommodation processes continue. By the time a child approaches age two, sensorimotor learning becomes less influential. Children act like what Piaget termed little scientists, engaging in trial-and-error experimentation, but are also able to use mental representations to predict outcomes. The child is capable of anticipating consequences that correspond with combining more than one mental representation. In this way, he or she begins to build a framework for navigating the physical and social environment.

Preoperational Thought

Before age six, children have not developed the ability to undergo logical reasoning. During this time of preoperational thought, children acquire language and necessary skills for social interactions. With ongoing experiences, they make gradual adjustments to accommodate what they know with what they have learned. Much of the knowledge acquired in early childhood develops out of play and through observation of others. Children are egocentric, focused on their own perspectives. Around the time children turn three, they begin to recognize that others have different views from their own. The idea that other people might think about the same things differently is called theory of mind. Social interactions provide a natural learning environment. Children who frequently interact with other children, have older siblings, and are frequently talked to especially by mothers or primary care givers, tend to develop a theory of mind sooner than do those without these interactions. The timing for achieving cognitive benchmarks, such as a theory of mind and logical reasoning, correlate with participation opportunities. For example, three-year-old children as well as six-year-old children recognize that a slide is something to sit on and ride down regardless of the size. Older children, unlike the three-year-old child, will make scale adjustments; they know it is impossible to slide down a four-inch miniature version of a playground slide.

Errors in logical reasoning are primarily due to centration, or the preoperational child's focus on a single characteristic. Children's knowledge is based on observable characteristics such as appearance, function, and their previous experiences, and before age six most will fail at reversibility and conservation tasks. Piaget's classic experiments demonstrate that by simply changing the shape or appearance of liquid, clay, or a row of items, young children fail to reason that amount or quantity remains the same. A change in appearance is a permanent change in the object, and the child believes that if it looks bigger, there is more. Before age six, children's thoughts are also limited by static reasoning, and they struggle to accept that things have been different from what they know them to be. For example, most young children find it shocking to learn that their parent was a baby at one time. They believe that things have always been the way things are now. As children move closer to school age, experience helps them gain more understanding about their environment. They move away from egocentrism and begin to use simple logic based on acquired knowledge.

Concrete Operational Thought

After age six, most children have reached a new cognitive benchmark and can apply logical reasoning with concrete information. Concrete information is factual knowledge based on the child's accumulated experiences. Because, around the world, almost all children of this age are in school, this period of growth is nurtured in both the academic and play setting where classification and sorting skills are practiced frequently.

Concrete operational children form new knowledge using inductive thought. In other words, they begin with what they know, and then work to find a solution or a new outcome. Neither concrete nor preoperational groups can apply logical reasoning in hypothetical situations; however, children with concrete reasoning skills can make inferences that align with what they know is true. For example, if given 10 sticks that vary in length and asked to align them in order by length, younger children (under six) will engage in trial and error, such as laying down the sticks and arranging them one by one to determine closeness of size. Older children will rely on strategy, such as holding all the sticks in their grasp, resting them on a level surface, and selecting them by length. Between ages 7 and 11, children begin to use problem-solving strategies, make scale adjustments, and perform reversibility tasks. These children can perform conservation tasks and can use classification and seriation techniques. In addition, these children are capable of transitive inference, a precursor to abstract thought processes. They can infer implied facts and can make conclusions based on relationships known about other facts, even though the details have not been stated. The limitations in logical reasoning help explain why these age groups characteristically place emphasis on their own perspectives and immediate appearance or function to explain what they know. However, as the child moves closer to adolescence, these characteristics diminish.

Formal Operational Thought

Children 12 and older progressively begin using deductive thinking strategies. That is, they begin with an idea and begin to apply logical and hypothetical principles to it to prove or disprove the idea. Initially, children begin to look at relationships between two things or concepts. Hypothetical thinking is a primary benchmark of formal operational intelligence and initiates advances in decision making for the adolescent mind. Adolescents use analytical (hypothetical-deductive) and intuitive thinking strategies to make decisions. As they move into late adolescence, they can look at multiple relationships. However, when emotions are present, adolescents are more likely to base a decision on a "gut feeling." In younger adolescents, emotional thinking occurs in place of analytical thinking, but older adolescents are capable of simultaneously using both types. Illogical reasoning gives way to rational thinking, and while adolescents overcome challenges of centration, they face new challenges related to egocentrism associated with identity development. Young adolescents think intensely about themselves and about what others think of them. Adolescents believe they are unique, special, and more socially significant than they actually are. The prefrontal cortex is still under development, and adolescents are more impulsive, shortsighted, and self-centered in decision making than the young adult.

Piaget's theory strongly emphasizes brain maturity and intellectual development resulting from assimilation and accommodation of information with existing schemas. He holds that lack of experience and the lack of neural pathways explain why children make mistakes in logical thinking and reasoning more than adults do. Magnetic resonance imaging (MRI) has helped researchers gain a better understanding of how much development continues through adolescence and into emerging adulthood. Several cortical areas undergo growth, making higher cognitive processes possible. Planning, organizing self-control, judgment, and emotional regulation integrate information from multiple areas of the brain. New developments in these intricate processes lead to changes in the perspectives on relationships with family and peers, identity, religion, politics, and moral reasoning.

Piaget's theory of child cognitive development is a relevant foundation for ongoing research today. A primary limitation is that there are variations in the age of cognitive benchmark attainment. Today's infants, children, adolescents, and young adults are capable of cognitive tasks earlier than what Piaget's model suggests. Likewise, there is much variability in cognitive abilities and declines across the adult life span. Some researchers have emphasized that cultural practices determine what tasks are learned, as well as the timing for learning them.

Multiple-Choice Questions

342. Piaget asserted that people form _____ of the world and how it works, based on their experiences in it.

(A) stereotypes
(B) attributions
(C) representations
(D) judgments

343. Adapting current intellect by making sense of new information based on existing knowledge is

(A) assimilation
(B) schema
(C) accommodation
(D) judgments

344. Constructing new mental representations from existing ones to include new experiences is

(A) assimilation
(B) schema
(C) accommodation
(D) judgments

345. Piaget believed the infant's participation, emotional expression, and focused attention in peek-a-boo games are indicative of early signs of _____ in which the infant actively tries to make events last.

(A) assimilation
(B) purposeful intention
(C) accommodation
(D) reflexes

346. Piaget thought children learned like _____, engaging in trial-and-error experimentation, using mental representations to predict outcomes and build a framework for navigating the physical and social environment.

(A) little scientists
(B) apprentices in learning
(C) little adults
(D) preoperational

347. What is the period of cognitive development in which Piaget noted that children's illogical reasoning is centered on observable characteristics such as appearance, function, and previous experiences?

(A) Little scientists
(B) Apprentices in learning
(C) Little adults
(D) Preoperational

348. A hallmark of adolescent cognitive development is the ability to reason based on propositions and possibilities rather than concrete facts, known as _____.

(A) inductive reasoning
(B) deductive reasoning
(C) hypothetical reasoning
(D) preoperational reasoning

Fill-in-the-Blank Questions

349. The four periods of cognitive development according to Piaget are _____, _____, _____, and _____.

350. In the first two stages of _____, the infant acquires first experiences and gains understanding of initially reflexive behaviors to create and strengthen sensory and motor neural communication pathways.

351. The idea that other people might think about the same things differently is called _____.

352. Errors in logical reasoning are primarily due to _____, or the preoperational child's focus on a single characteristic.

353. _____ uses implied inferences and conclusions based on relationships known about other facts, even though all the details are not provided.

354. Piaget believed children are capable of hypothetical thought in the _____ period of cognitive development.

355. Adolescents are capable of using _____ and _____ thinking strategies when making decisions.

Short-Answer Questions

356. Describe the relationship between oral stimulation (sucking, biting, tasting) and infant cognition.

357. Explain the changes in infant intelligence during the sensorimotor period according to Piaget.

358. Describe the factors that influence how soon a child acquires theory of mind.

359. Before age six, most children will fail at reversibility and conservation tasks. Why?

360. Between ages 7 and 12, children gain and improve in metacognition and metamemory skills. These children are in Piaget's concrete operational period of intellectual development in which children are capable of logical reasoning on observable facts (not hypothetical). Explain how the principles of the information processing theory complement cognitive advancements that occur during this period.

361. Describe the differences between analytic thinking and intuitive thinking, and explain why adolescents tend to use intuitive thinking to a greater extent than analytic thinking.

362. Describe the influence of egocentrism on reasoning during adolescence.

Sociocultural Learning

Lev Vygotsky (1896–1934), a Russian psychologist, introduced a cultural perspective to cognitive development, suggesting that beyond the biology of brain maturation, social learning is central to cognition. Vygotsky proposed that children learn within a social context and that what they learn in this context influences how they think as they mature. In other words, knowledge gained through social interactions, such as play and responsibilities, helps advance cognitive reasoning. Culture, according to Vygotsky, determines what is important for the child to learn, and children will learn what is necessary for transitioning into adulthood within their cultures. He viewed language as the primary mediator for the child's understanding and learning and communication as key in bringing about learning.

Vygotsky explained that early in childhood, as children begin forming new words, they engage in private speech, or they narrate actions, thoughts, and intentions much like a screenplay. Private speech is children's way of processing what they are doing, what they want to do, and the effect of what they have done. After age six, children use fewer words in their private speech. Vygotsky believed this is a transition period where children begin to use internal self-talk. Around age eight, most of the self-talk is internalized; however, even adults talk aloud to themselves when working through a problem or task. Private speech gives way to organized thinking and becomes part of executive problem-solving skills as seen in adolescence.

Everyone experiences a learning curve, or a period when practice is necessary to execute a new task independently and correctly. Vygotsky categorized learning as tasks and skills outside of the child's immediate potential, tasks that can be done with assistance, and tasks that can be done independently. Vygotsky described tasks that cannot be performed independently but are within one's potential as being in the individual's zone of proximal development. Vygotsky considered children as apprentices in learning and held that adults (parents, teachers, and mentors) are crucial in guiding children through their zone of proximal development. Vygotsky referred to this temporary support as scaffolding. Parents and other mentors provide scaffolding until the child masters the task.

Vygotsky's and Piaget's theories of cognitive development are complementary. Both Piaget and Vygotsky focused on child cognitive development, emphasizing that language development in early childhood is closely tied to cognitive abilities, and that children are active participants in their learning experiences. The primary differences between Piaget's and Vygotsky's perspectives are that Piaget believed cognition developed in periods associated with age that allowed particular types of learning to advance, while Vygotsky believed cognition developed because of learning experiences, extending Piaget's work to include how the individual learns from interactions with other children and adults from their culture. Vygotsky and Piaget both viewed children as eager and active learners.

Multiple-Choice Questions

363. _____ is children's way of processing what they are doing, what they want to do, and the effect of what they have done.

(A) Private speech
(B) Attributions
(C) Social context
(D) Social learning

364. _____ is essential in Piaget's theory of social learning, and communication is key in bringing about learning.

(A) Private speech
(B) Language
(C) Social context
(D) Reinforcements

365. According to Vygotsky, children learn by interacting with a mentor to accomplish a task, or _____.

(A) preschool
(B) language
(C) social context
(D) guided participation

366. Vygotsky emphasized that children will gain the knowledge that is valued within their _____.

(A) preschool
(B) language
(C) social context
(D) zone of proximal development

367. Which of the following is not an area of social exchange that advances cognitive reasoning?

(A) Informal communication
(B) Formal communication
(C) Reading
(D) Heredity

368. Vygotsky emphasized the role of _____, in contrast to Piaget's emphasis on brain maturation.

(A) sociocultural context
(B) formal communication
(C) guided participation
(D) zone of proximal development

369. Mindy can dress herself each day, but she cannot tie her shoes, zip her zipper, or button her shirts. For Mindy, dressing is in her _____ because she has the potential to dress herself, but she is not doing so completely without assistance.

    (A) sociocultural context
    (B) formal communication
    (C) guided participation
    (D) zone of proximal development

Fill-in-the-Blank Questions

370. _____ proposed that social learning is central to cognition.

371. Vygotsky emphasized that _____ was critical for thinking, whereas Piaget held that brain maturation and experiences mattered most.

372. Within the social learning theory, _____ are the child's first mentors.

373. Tasks that cannot be performed independently but are within a child's potential are in the child's _____.

374. Vygotsky referred to the temporary assistance provided by parents and other mentors until the child masters the task as _____.

375. Vygotsky and Piaget shared the belief that children are _____ in their learning experiences.

376. Private speech promotes organized thinking and becomes part of _____ in adolescence.

377. Vygotsky referred to children as _____ as they engage in social interactions throughout their day.

Short-Answer Questions

378. Explain the similarities and differences between Vygotsky and Piaget on cognitive development in childhood.

379. Explain the zone of proximal development. Provide an example.

380. Describe some of the principles of Vygotsky's theory of sociocultural learning.

381. According to Vygotsky, what should parents and other caregivers do to encourage a child's learning about healthy eating?

382. Describe the role of scaffolding in childhood cognitive development.

383. According to Vygotsky, how does culture contribute to a child's cognitive development?

Kohlberg's Moral Reasoning

Young children are initially driven to gratify their needs and wants. Parents guide children toward delaying gratification and in prioritizing needs and wants as appropriate to valued social norms. Society or culture provides the framework of beliefs as to what is morally right or wrong and continues to shape and influence moral development throughout one's life. While the psychoanalytical perspective introduced insights of the biological and unconscious motives that drive behaviors, social psychologists highlighted the importance of culture, and cognitive psychologists provided an intellectual framework for understanding childhood decision making. Therefore development of moral reasoning can be considered across the paradigms.

Lawrence Kohlberg (1927–1987) provided a model to measure developmental changes in moral thinking across ages. Kohlberg presented the participants, male adolescents from upper-middle-class homes, with a scenario about a man Heinz and his terminally ill wife. In summary, the moral dilemma is that the man cannot afford the medication his wife needs to get better, and without it she will die, so he breaks into the pharmacy and steals the medicine. The participants were asked if they think Heinz should have done it, and why or why not.

Kohlberg explained that up until about age five, or school age, children lack moral reasonability. During early childhood, children do not think about rules in their daily actions. Few will understand that rules are necessary standards of behaviors, and they are more likely to create rules that help them reach their goals. This changes around the time children begin attending school, and rules become important. Kohlberg proposed three levels of moral reasoning and six stages within each level. The three levels, preconventional, conventional, and postconventional, are associated with the stages of cognitive development as proposed by Piaget.

At the preconventional level, children are egocentric, as Piaget described preoperational children to be. They start out with goals to be good and want to be recognized for making the good decision. Children move from obeying rules to avoid punishment (stage 1) to consider fairness and negotiation (stage 2). The first stage of preconventional moral reasoning is when children view authority figures as in charge of rules, and to the child, the rules are literal. In stage 2, children begin to weigh in their own interest in deciding to follow the rules. Children want to avoid getting into trouble as much as possible, and consider rule breaking as something bad. However, as children move into middle childhood, they become less egocentric and begin to see reasons for breaking the rules, though the goal to avoid trouble does not change, and they do their best to avoid being caught.

As children move into adolescence, hormonal changes increase emotional reasoning, or intuitive thinking, and there is a greater likelihood that feelings will influence decisions about right and wrong. As adolescents transition through stages 3 and 4 of the conventional level, they begin to consider the needs of others over their black-and-white boundaries of right and wrong. In doing so, they exhibit increased prosocial behaviors of forgiveness and generosity. For example, children begin to recognize that others may have a disadvantage, and many will naturally offer extra help or make exceptions to the rule in such situations. By late adolescence, appreciation of rules deepens as teenagers recognize the importance of social order for the good of the group, not just the person. As they move into early adulthood, there is an expectation that everyone's benefit should be considered in the decision rather than that of just one individual. Teamwork and loyalty to the group are valued more than individual interests or goals.

Young adults mature in moral reasoning to varying degrees; however, for most the postconventional level of moral development is not acquired until later in adulthood, and many adults do not function at these higher levels. The last two stages may not differ in final solutions or decision; however, the reasoning behind the decision represents a different agenda. While many adults are content with perspectives of justice, oriented around laws and individual rights (stage 5), others take a global perspective in which universal principles of fairness are emphasized (stage 6).

Transitioning through the levels of moral reasoning as proposed by Kohlberg depends on experiences, including reinforcements and punishment, but also on cognitive maturation. Initial transition of adolescents into independent young adult roles involves an integration of the shared beliefs of the parental environment and aspects of the new social environment. Most adults recognize there is value in being flexible and open to change, and they are therefore motivated to compromise. In addition, many realize that more involvement with diverse cultures broadens individual perspective, and therefore promotes better adaptation into diverse social roles.

Beliefs and values are subject to social norms, which are further influenced by culture. Culture can include peer, religious, or ethnic groups. Kohlberg's theory has been criticized for not taking into account the differences across cultures as well as between genders.

Moral reasoning models are useful in practice; they provide a base to measure and predict behaviors. The three levels of moral reasoning are comparable to levels of personal, communal, and universal morality. While age often predicts moral judgment levels, chronological age is not the determining variable. Culture, experience, and biological variables are significant determiners in advancing moral judgment.

Multiple-Choice Questions

384. _____ influence(s) how quickly children progress through each stage of Kohlberg's morality development.

(A) Stereotypes
(B) Reinforcements
(C) Age
(D) Judgments

385. According to Kohlberg's theory, moral decisions are made by using principles that reflect core values in the _____ stage of development.

(A) preconventional
(B) conventional
(C) postconventional
(D) formal conventional

386. The stage of Kohlberg's morality theory in which decisions are based on avoiding punishment for rule breaking and being seen as bad is the _____ stage.

(A) preconventional
(B) conventional
(C) postconventional
(D) formal conventional

387. Forgiveness and generosity are characteristics of decision making in the _____ stage of Kohlberg's morality theory.

(A) preconventional
(B) conventional
(C) postconventional
(D) formal conventional

388. Trish turns down a cigarette offered by her friend Amanda, stating that smoking is wrong and she does not want to get into trouble. Trish's decision is characteristic of _____ reasoning.

(A) preconventional
(B) conventional
(C) postconventional
(D) formal conventional

389. Cognitive development resulting from _____ strongly influences moral reasoning in adulthood.

    (A) experiences
    (B) attributions
    (C) punishments
    (D) judgments

390. An adolescent in Piaget's concrete operational stage is most likely in Kohlberg's _____ moral reasoning.

    (A) preconventional
    (B) conventional
    (C) postconventional
    (D) formal conventional

Fill-in-the-Blank Questions

391. _____ expanded on the work of Piaget and created a model demonstrating how morality develops and progresses from childhood through adulthood.

392. The level of moral reasoning, according to Kohlberg, in which children are egocentric and focus only on the good side of morality is the _____ stage.

393. Young school-age children emphasize wrong and right until experience teaches them to consider _____.

394. Moral reasoning in the preconventional stage is characterized by acknowledging right and wrong and preferring to be seen as a good person. Children are more likely to break the rules when _____.

395. As adolescents transition into young adulthood, they move away from being egocentric and toward a deeper appreciation for the benefit of the group. Growing concern for social order is characteristic of _____ moral reasoning.

396. When asked if Heinz should have broken into the pharmacy and stolen the medication, individuals in the _____ level would likely answer that Heinz did the right thing because his wife deserved the medication.

397. Moral reasoning in adulthood depends on the _____ the adult assumes.

Short-Answer Questions

398. Explain how children develop moral reasoning according to Kohlberg.

399. Describe how adolescents differ from children in moral reasoning.

400. According to Kohlberg, what influences transitions of moral development from adolescence to adulthood?

401. Describe the difference in perspectives for adult moral reasoning in the postconventional stage.

402. In what ways do Kohlberg's levels of moral reasoning parallel with Piaget's periods of cognitive development?

403. What are some of the limitations of Kohlberg's theory of moral reasoning?

404. Sharing prescription medications is illegal and can be very dangerous. Yet, many people share medications despite the warnings or potential legal consequences. Studies show a large number of adolescents regularly share prescription medications too (Daniel, Honein, and Moore, 2003). Using Kohlberg's model of moral reasoning, discuss potential reasoning of adolescents (ages 9 to 17).

Schaie: Intelligence and Cognition in Adulthood

Much of the frameworks for adult cognition orients around intelligence, emphasizing decline and compensation processes. However, some theorists propose a fifth level of cognition to help with understanding what influences changes in cognition. Postformal thought models highlight the qualitative changes of adult cognition and logical thinking as one ages. Adults grow increasingly flexible in applying logic to problems while at the same time taking into consideration multiple, and often opposing, perspectives.

As the founder of the Seattle Longitudinal Study (1956), K. Warner Schaie (1928–) has been instrumental in expanding perspectives on adult intelligence. Schaie explored trends in adult intelligence scores for four decades, examining variables that influence changes in cognitive processes as people age. The study demonstrated how health and personality influence the absence or presence of age-related cognitive changes, differences, as well as the magnitude. In his theory, he described seven stages in which cognitive functioning transforms or adapts during adulthood in response to the new responsibilities and pressures. Age correlates with various daily living milestones, and therefore much of what makes up a person's intelligence phenotype is age specific (Schaie & Willis, 2000). Schaie proposes that new roles, along with the corresponding needs and responsibilities, lead to shifts in cognition preparing the person for the next level of cognitive functioning.

The first three stages, acquisition, achieving, and responsible, represent transitions or shifts in mental focus from self-serving to social responsibilities. Throughout most of adolescence, many teenagers have modest amounts of responsibilities and are protected from the demands and pressures associated with adult decision making. However, adolescence is a time when brain maturity allows for a vast amount of new information to be stored and utilized. However, because adolescents are egocentric in thinking, most of this information is self-serving and unrelated to practical, long-term goals. Schaie referred to adolescence as a stage of acquisition, in which experiences create shifts in cognition that prepare the adolescent brain to advance in using information. In other words, the accumulation of new knowledge and skills during adolescence promotes adjusting to the cognitive pressures and demands of emerging adulthood.

Schaie explained emerging adulthood as a time for achieving; a time when information is adapted to plan and solve problems to meet long-term goals for livelihood. Young adults are accountable for the consequences of their decisions, but they struggle because most of the important decisions they need to make about career, relationships, and self-care do not have concrete answers or clearly defined steps for achievement. Decision making continues to be focused on filling self-needs but also starts to include the need of others, or social responsibilities. The responsibility stage allows the adult to practice alternate approaches to achieving goals, including acknowledging others' perspectives.

In the executive stage, adults begin to integrate perspectives and develop complex relationships. Conflict resolution and problem-solving abilities mature. Between early and middle adulthood, goals become highly structured and contain social practicality. It is during these years that adults become concerned with more than just their own survival. Family, community, and work are important aspects of individual goals.

As adults grow older, skills required to reach goals become more refined. Age and experience make it easier for an adult to narrow in alternative approaches, and better direct their focus. Schaie considers older adulthood a stage of reorganization because older adults must be more flexible in finding ways to have meaningful experiences. Practical knowledge dominates daily events, and older adults rely less on planning and organizing efforts when setting and achieving goals. Many know from experience how to measure the worth of a goal against the mental and physical effort necessary to reach it. As older adults move into the elderly years, much of the mental functions are focused on day-to-day activities and relationships. In this stage of reintegration, the most concerning events are what is relevant in the present, or the very near future. Therefore, fewer cognitive efforts are directed toward problem solving, unless the problem is critical to daily activities. Elderly adults prioritize mental or physical energy on events that hold immediate importance.

There is a great deal of variance in health and independence status among early and late adult age groups. Chronological age is not a determining factor; however, particular transitions are common within age groups, which create social norms. Social norms strongly influence goal pursuits at every age. Schaie described the final stage of cognitive functioning as legacy-leaving, and he suggests that this stage is characteristic of an individual approaching end of life, whose mind is sound but body is frail. Timing of transition into the last stage greatly depends on one's health status and awareness of physiological decline. Elderly adults seem to direct cognitive efforts toward sharing memories and passing on knowledge in hopes to continue the meaningfulness of one's life into the next generation.

Schaie's theory focuses on how the adult responds to pressures of increasing responsibilities common to Western cultures. The seven stages of cognitive functioning may not be relevant within other cultures, and the order of the functions may not be the same for all older adults. However, relevant to all adult cognitive models is that what is necessary for survival in one's environment tends to become a social norm for cognitive functioning.

Multiple-Choice Questions

405. Who is the researcher who proposed that new roles, along with the corresponding needs and responsibilities, influence intellectual functioning and therefore lead to changes in cognition?

(A) K. Warner Schaie
(B) Lawrence Kohlberg
(C) Lev Vygotsky
(D) Jean Piaget

406. The long-term study on adult intelligence emphasizing changes in cognitive processes as people age is the

(A) Theory of Moral Reasoning
(B) Study of Emerging Reflection
(C) Seattle Longitudinal Study
(D) Longitudinal Study of Intelligence and Aging

407. According to Schaie, _____ and _____ determine age-related changes in cognitive functioning.

(A) health and education
(B) health and career
(C) health and personality
(D) health and marital status

408. What is the stage of cognitive growth when newly acquired information is vast and self-serving, not connected directly to long-term goals?

(A) Reintegration
(B) Acquisition
(C) Responsibility
(D) Executive

409. Flexibility for problem solving and setting and planning goals are characteristic of the _____ stage.

(A) reintegration
(B) reorganization
(C) responsibility
(D) legacy-leaving

410. The stage in which older adults prioritize mental energy for important events and daily activities is _____.

(A) reintegration
(B) reorganization
(C) responsibility
(D) legacy-leaving

411. What is the stage in which cognitive energies are focused on sharing memories and passing on knowledge for the approaching end-of-life transition?

(A) Reintegration
(B) Reorganization
(C) Responsibility
(D) Legacy-leaving

Fill-in-the-Blank Questions

412. The _____demonstrated that health and personality influence the absence or presence of age-related cognitive changes, differences, as well as the magnitude.

413. Adult cognition grows in response to _____, in which finding a solution to various problems in life requires a person to expand his or her perspective.

414. Schaie explains that adolescent and young adult cognition shifts from _____, gaining and storing a lot of information based on one's interest without accountability, to _____, focusing on goals and planning for long-range roles and dealing with the consequences of decisions.

415. Schaie proposed that expectations and goals for adults vary because _____ have a strong influence on cognitive development at every age.

416. Setting well-structured and practical goals is characteristic of adult cognition in the _____ stage.

417. In the _____ stage, emphasis is placed on sharing memories and passing on knowledge in hopes to continue the meaningfulness of one's life into the next generation.

418. Particular transitions common within age groups create social norms that influence goal pursuits. Transition and progression through the final stages of Schaie's model is determined by _____.

Short-Answer Questions

419. Describe activities characteristic of the acquisition and achieving stages that prepare an adult for typical social roles in the responsibility stage.

420. Explain characteristics of the executive stage of Schaie's theory on adult cognition.

421. Explain Schaie's perspective on the influences that bring changes in adult thinking.

422. Explain a limitation of Schaie's stage theory.

Postformal Thought: Cognition and Moral Reasoning in Young Adulthood

Perry: Transition from Dualism to Relativism

William G. Perry (1913–1998) focused his research on understanding how cognition and moral development changes in college students. College provides a unique growth opportunity that accelerates intellectual development. As Kohlberg demonstrated, improved intellectual functioning generates changes in moral reasoning. Perry proposed a stage theory in which cognition continually advances from extreme dualism to high levels of personally committed beliefs, or relativism. He considered each advancement to be a position of postformal thought.

The first four positions are dominated by dualistic thoughts, with the first being extremely right or wrong thinking. Position 1, strict dualism, implies a rigid adherence to authority figures, and Perry asserted that no one enters college at this level. Very few young adults do not question at least some of the information coming from authority figures.

The next three include degrees of multiplicity, where young adults begin to question the accuracy of the information given by authority figures. The second position is prelegitimate multiplicity, characterized by having many ideas, answers to questions, and points of view. In this stage, individuals are aware that some of the information available to them is right and that they have to go through it to discover the truth. The common belief among early college students is that general education courses unrelated to their chosen degree are a waste of time is an example of emerging multiplicity. Position 3, early multiplicity, is characterized by the belief that more than one idea may be correct. For the student, this is typically discovered at the point in college where evaluating information is necessary to achieve the grade outcomes they want. While students acknowledge that there are multiple perspectives, they believe that only some of the perspectives are accurate or relevant. Furthermore, even though students and young adults expect that validating information with evidence is important, at this point outside assistance with evaluating information and formulating an accurate solution is necessary. In position 4, late multiplicity, students become better at deciphering information based on relevancy and accepting that even experts have unique perspectives that often differ from one another. Rationalizing information, constructing and evaluating arguments, is the final transition before students acquire relativism.

Positions 5 through 9 are dominated by relativism, and adults begin to be open to the opinions of others. They have stronger abilities to evaluate information for accuracy and have an increased preference for a worldview perspective. Relativism begins as contextual relativism, where acceptance of truth depends on where it comes from and how it affects the student. Even at this early stage of relativism, students can identify with chosen authority figures as colleagues in the same endeavors. At the position 6 level, commitment foreseen, young adults begin to identify with particular aspects of themselves. They have gained enough information to base long-term decisions such as making commitments to career, religion, political, and personal areas of their life. Adults changing, adapting, and accommodating new perspectives with their own characterize positions 7 through 9. Individuals move from an initial commitment, then transition to multiple commitments, and then transition to a state of resolve. Considering others' perspectives helps young adults begin to commit to their own personal beliefs. In addition, as commitment grows, adults are able to return to dualistic thinking in order to evaluate information that conflicts with personal beliefs. Being able to retreat from conflicting information will temporarily allow adults to delay making a decision about the accuracy of the information.

Perry's theory has been criticized because it is exceptionally comprehensive. It incorporates cognitive and moral theories as well as identity and personality theories. However, it is popular because it provides a way to assess problem-solving characteristics. Dualistic thinkers are more likely to take a narrow approach, breaking down events into discrete tasks. Relativists are more likely to approach the problem as whole and to utilize evidence-based information to support their thinking and problem solving.

Kitchener: Emergence of Reflective Judgment

Karen Strohm Kitchener (1943–) and colleagues proposed a stage model explaining moral reasoning as the process of reflective judgment. Kitchener believed many decisions faced by adults are in the form of a moral dilemma. Kitchener's seven-stage theory suggests there are three dimensions that adults progress through as they make decisions: certainty of knowledge, processes used to acquire knowledge, and the kind of evidence used to justify one's judgments to explain how adults analyze problems and justify their problem solving.

The first three stages are based on certainty: single concrete instances, right or wrong answers, and progressing to awareness that while some types of knowledge are certain, other types may be uncertain. Because knowledge is based on single concrete instances, individuals' judgments are limited to experience and are biased by self-perspective. Stages 4 and 5 are characterized by the individual becoming more flexible in perspective. While personal opinions and beliefs remain dominant influences, there is an awareness that there are other perspectives and that some people will make decisions based on differing viewpoints. Judgments made from reflective thinking, based on experiences combined with learned rules and strategies, emerge in the later stages as individuals begin to weigh in evidence with personal beliefs. Advance reflective thinking accepts that while some types of knowledge are uncertain, evidence, such as research findings, shows that there is a chance the information is true.

Kitchener's and Perry's stage theories emphasize how life experiences advance cognitive growth in young adult years, and particularly in response to educational experience. Progression toward reflective judgment in real-life settings is not quick. For example, relativism is characteristic of middle-age adults. Young adults are more likely to hold to a belief that an absolute truth is possible.

Multiple-Choice Questions

423. _____ proposed a stage theory in which cognition continually advances from extreme dualism to high levels of personally committed beliefs, or relativism.

(A) Karen Strohm Kitchener
(B) K. Warner Schaie
(C) William Perry
(D) Lawrence Kohlberg

424. Which of the following is not a level of intellectual transition according to Perry?

(A) Acquisition
(B) Dualism
(C) Multiplicity
(D) Relativism

425. What is the second level of intellectual transition in which young adults come to realize there is more than one perspective and begin to prioritize based on fact and strength of support?

(A) Acquisition
(B) Dualism
(C) Multiplicity
(D) Relativism

426. Relativism is _____ when acceptance of truth depends on where it comes from and how it affects the student.

(A) acquisition
(B) dualistic
(C) contextual
(D) accurate

427. Reflective judgment is a _____ for problem solving, resulting from concrete knowledge, flexibility in thinking, and reflecting on experiences.

(A) judgment
(B) working model
(C) strategy
(D) solution

428. The idea that adult judgments related to morality and other life decisions progress through seven stages of knowledge and reflection was proposed by _____.

(A) William Perry
(B) K. Warner Schaie
(C) Lawrence Kohlberg
(D) Karen Strohm Kitchener

429. Kitchener and Perry both believe that awareness of others' _____ is important in advancing cognition.

(A) perspective
(B) judgments
(C) authority
(D) none of the above

Fill-in-the-Blank Questions

430. Perry's perspective of advancing awareness and acceptance of transitions in knowledge (fixed, absolute, and contextual) is a theory of _____.

431. Perry emphasized the role of college in accelerating _____.

432. Before acquiring _____, a young adult must be able to rationalize information, construct, and evaluate arguments.

433. In the advanced stage of relativistic thought, when there is conflicting information, adults are able to _____ to resolve dilemmas.

434. The _____ model is a seven-stage theory describing how adults analyze elements of a problem and justify their problem solving.

435. Certainty of knowledge in reflective judgments is limited because it comes from _____ and is biased by self-perspective.

436. Having awareness of others' perspectives and accepting that others will make decisions based on their perspective demonstrates _____ in Kitchener's reflective judgment stage theory.

437. Using experiences combined with _____ is characteristic of the most advanced level in reflective judgment.

Short-Answer Questions

438. Describe the first four positions of postformal thought.

439. Describe positions five through nine of postformal thought and highlight the transitions in perspectives.

440. Describe the approaches to problem solving for dualistic and relativistic thinkers.

441. Describe the three dimensions in Kitchener's stage theory of reflective judgment.

442. According to Perry and Kitchener, how do young adults become relativist thinkers? How might relativistic thinking benefit a health professional?

443. Explain the influence of level of cognitive reasoning on an individual's openness to intervention/prevention strategies.

CHAPTER 6

Social Theories and Perspectives

Social Cognition

Social cognition, or the way we come to understand others, begins developing in childhood. Social roles, interactions, and relationships help us interpret, analyze, remember, and use information about our social worlds. In this way, we form mental representations and frameworks for how we live our life from day to day. People are in a constant state of social interaction and rely on a normative influence, a standard of knowledge about which behaviors are acceptable in social settings and relationships, to gain acceptance and approval.

Social norms are unwritten but established rules that govern social behaviors. Cultural social norms provide heuristics, which are standard representations to be applied when understanding complex information. The more similar the new situation or information is to the stored heuristic, the more confident people feel about their action or judgment. For example, people are more likely to side with the majority when they do not understand the information presented to them. Siding with the majority provides a sometimes false sense of accuracy based on the idea that a belief is better if a greater number of members subscribe to it. While not always accurate, established schemas and perceived reliable heuristics influence future behaviors and predictions about future events. Unfortunately, predictions based on previous experience increase the risk of self-fulfillment, or taking actions that increase the likelihood of an outcome. Self-fulfilling prophecies are predictions that make themselves come true because people engage in behaviors under the expectation of a particular outcome.

When faced with conflicting information, people tend to rely on available heuristic strategies. In other words, when something unexpected happens, people try to make sense of it based on stored information that is easily recalled and is in some way connected to the situation. Furthermore, people can generalize meanings, which makes some responses seem automatic, such as stereotypes. Stereotyping is the process of making inferences based on group categorical information, such as ethnicity, age, location, and religion. Unfortunately, stereotypes lead to inaccurate judgments because people tend to perceive everything within the group as being the same or closely related and very different from everything outside of the group. In addition, any deviance from the stereotype is justified by making an exception with the group. Subtyping is the process of modifying the stereotype belief without completely abandoning it.

Judgments about others are necessary for human survival, and therefore, accuracy is important. Humans need each other to provide resources that promote survival, mate selection, and reproduction. Therefore, it is important to feel confident in the accuracy of judgments made about the safety, reliability, and dependability of social environments.

Biases and Errors in Social Cognition

Stereotyping is strongly connected to attributions, or inferences we make about the things other people do. Typically, we attribute behaviors to either the situation or the individual's disposition; however, attributions are prone to bias and error. The fundamental attribution error states that we are more likely to attribute others' behaviors to a disposition, even if it was triggered by the situation. Interestingly, the same bias is not true about self-attributions. The actor-observer effect states that people will attribute others' actions as dispositional and their own as situational, even when the behavior is identical. This bias is made because the situational effect has a mental connection that is invisible to the observer unless additional mental effort is put forth by the observer to make the inferred connections. Since it is much easier to make the dispositional attribution, one must be motivated to make a situational attribution.

Multiple-Choice Questions

444. Someone considering a career in social psychology is interested in understanding _____.

(A) the patterns of diversity in population growth
(B) how people developed from childhood into adulthood
(C) what people think and how they act when they are in social settings
(D) the influence of heredity on gene expression for the extrovert personality trait

445. Our likes and dislikes, and favorable or unfavorable evaluations of and reactions to objects, people, situations, or other aspects of the world refer to _____.

(A) values
(B) attitudes
(C) social cognition
(D) personality

446. The assessments and evaluations we make about other people's behavior are known as _____.

(A) stereotypes
(B) attributions
(C) schemas
(D) judgments

447. Awareness of expected behaviors and interactions in relationships with others refers to _____.

(A) social etiquette
(B) social cognition
(C) cognitive dissonance
(D) stereotypes

448. Someone who understands what another's behaviors are like and uses this information to explain why he or she behaves in a certain way is relying on _____.

(A) social influence
(B) attribution theory
(C) self-serving bias
(D) social cognition

449. People use past information or _____ to help them make sense of new social experiences.

(A) stereotypes
(B) attributions
(C) schemas
(D) judgments

450. Most people can pull up a general schema for the word *person*; however, when we think of a particular type of person, such as a celebrity, we use a schema based on our ideas surrounding what a celebrity is like. This schema is also known as a/an _____.

(A) stereotype
(B) attribution
(C) schema
(D) judgment

Fill-in-the-Blank Questions

451. Stereotyping people by categorical groups causes us to _____ the similarities between groups.

452. The tendency to make dispositional attributions rather than situational attribution when evaluating others' behaviors is termed the _____ .

453. Stereotypes cause us to interpret others' actions with _____ and lead us to falsely believe those people conform to our stereotypes.

454. Bringing about a situation that one expects to see happen is the _____ .

455. Stereotyping by putting others into categories leads us to _____ the similarities within group.

456. Making modifications to, instead of canceling out, a stereotype is called _____ .

457. To understand the type of person someone is, we make _____ , or assertions about what a person did and why he or she did it.

Short-Answer Questions

458. Explain why people tend to subscribe to the majority group.

459. Distinguish between dispositional attributions and situational attributions in making inferences on the behavior of others.

460. Jessie's grandparents are elderly and require help from the family in order to continue living in their home. Jessie believes this is normal for elderly adults. An elderly couple recently moved into the house next door to Jessie. Jessie is shocked to see that they are always on the go, traveling, camping, and even riding bicycles on the city trails. Explain how Jessie might process this contradicting information.

Social Identity Theory

Psychologists spend a great deal of time understanding the nature of the "self," our sense of who we are, and exploring whether we have only one true self or many selves. Self-concept is defined along a personal and social continuum. Personal identity refers to one's perceived individuality and characteristics that are relatively constant, while social identity consists of group-specific characteristics. Everyone has a social identity, one that is defined by the members within a social context. The social identity theory suggests that within the group we belong to, people have a tendency to move toward others who are positive and well received and away from those who are negative and rejected by others.

Social identity is shaped through social comparisons and evaluation of group membership. Intragroup comparisons are judgments about similarities and differences within same-group members. Intergroup comparisons are judgments about similarities and differences between the members within one's group and those belonging to a different group. Both groups provide a situational context for defining oneself, how we perceive our self, and how we act in social settings. Because belonging and not belonging to a group can affect our self-esteem, self-definitions are subject to reinterpretation.

As individuals, how we define who we are depends on the situation, and we cannot experience each aspect of ourselves in any one moment. Because self-concept is defined within a context, self-identity is complexly organized by categories. For example, we belong to several groups, and each group role contributes to the self-identity. As our roles gain in importance or complexity, they become more distinct from our other role identities. Greater distinction allows each identity to exist in its context and provides protection for situations when significant revision (title change) happens; there will be little to no impact on the other aspects of one's self-concept. On the other hand, when the self has low complexity or identities are blended rather than distinct, and there is a greater overlap in different components of the self, a person will feel more stress to the overall sense of self should something negatively impact one of the identities.

In addition to the situation, how others treat us shapes our identity. When the self is at risk for rejection, people will change aspects of themselves to fit in better with the desired group, or they will make comparison judgments that confirm positive aspects of the traditional group. For example, how strongly one's identity is independent or interdependent is determined mostly by culture. Many people are multicultural and adjust their behaviors to fit within the norms of each group.

There are endless ways to achieve group membership, both natural and environmental. People can choose which crowd they want to belong to; however, ethnicity, gender, and age are static group traits. Belonging to one group often means rejecting and being rejected by another. Rejection triggers judgments or comparisons based on simple characteristics such as hairstyles, clothing brands or styles, and body art, which make statements about the group and its members. The more different the out-group is from the in-group, the more likely the rejection, especially when the out-group differs significantly from the wider culture's standards for normal, and when the differences are viewed negatively.

Any form of oppression or devaluation of humanity based on group belonging is a form of prejudice and discrimination. Prejudice is the feeling component of attitude toward social groups, and is based solely on a person's membership in a particular group. When disapproved actions are associated with a group other than one's own, people tend to attribute the undesired behaviors to the members of the group. Generalized attributions about a group based on the actions of one or more members is a form of prejudice. Prejudice implies that the attributes are permanent or unchanging aspects of the other. Some prejudicial beliefs are so strong that someone not belonging to the rejected group who interacts with members of that group is viewed negatively, or is contaminated by association. For example, groups, such as religious, political, and ethnic, often forbid intermarriage. In some cases, even friendships outside of one of these groups is forbidden. Fitting in is important for finding a niche within social systems, and social identities are always under construction, and the particular group one belongs to determines which characteristics are most valued or least desired. Group perspective leads to prejudice toward others outside the group, and prejudice can lead to discrimination and oppression.

Multiple-Choice Questions

461. Who we are based on the groups to which we belong refers to
_____.

(A) self-concept
(B) social identity
(C) social cognition
(D) ethnicity

462. We can describe our sense of self by making _____ comparisons, or comparisons with other people within the same group.

(A) stereotype
(B) race
(C) intragroup
(D) intergroup

463. What is the term used to describe one's attitude toward social groups based solely on a person's membership in a particular group?

(A) Stereotype
(B) Prejudice
(C) Intragroup
(D) Intergroup

464. People have _____ social identities, in which there could be different implications for behavior depending on the particular social setting.
    (A) multiple
    (B) complex
    (C) intragroup
    (D) intergroup

Fill-in-the-Blank Questions

465. Our sense of who we are is based on a continuum between our _____ unique characteristics and our _____ group membership identities.

466. In any given moment we define ourselves by who we are in a particular _____.

467. One way to define our social self is based on _____ comparisons, or by the ways the group we belong to differs from a group we do not belong to.

468. The degree of intergroup and intragroup influences on one's identity depends on _____.

Short-Answer Questions

469. Describe some characteristics that define personal identity, and some characteristics that define social identity.

470. Explain how a characteristic of the self, such as being organized, can be both true and false.

471. Separating self-identities can create a lot of stress when they conflict with each other. Why is it important to keep principal identities distinct from each other?

472. Explain the difference between individualistic and collectivist cultures on self-identity expectations.

Social Influence

Emotions are powerful influences on social cognition, and to avoid cognitive dissonance, people work to balance personal attitudes with social norms. Social norms are customary standards for behavior shared by members of a particular culture. Cultures and societies are bound together by a fundamental force: social influence. Social influence is the control of one person's behavior by another, and it is the reason people give their time, money, allegiance, or affection to another person. Without it, there would be no altruism or cooperation, and people would not be motivated to join groups.

Social influence works because people have three essential desires that can only be met through interactions with others. Humans are pleasure seeking, need others' approval, and strive to know the correct or right information. From birth, humans have a hedonic motive toward gratifying experiences, or to avoid pain as much as possible. People preserve their efforts to satisfy needs and desires. Rewards and punishments have powerful effects on shaping behaviors, and the influence can be achieved through observing others. Witnessing another person receive recognition for a particular action will increase motivation for one to attempt the action as well. Likewise, observing someone receive a reprimand for a particular behavior decreases another's motivation for that behavior. However, this is not a simple thought process because most of the time social influence comes at us from all directions. Furthermore, there are people who are challenged to achieve where others have failed, regardless of how severe the consequences of failure are.

People work hard to gain acceptance of the people around them. Acting in appropriate ways for the situation is a good place to start. Members of the group provide normative influence, information about behaviors that are appropriate for the group. The custom of saying please and thank you, opening and holding doors open, and exchanging gifts are behaviors influenced by member influence. In fact, reciprocity is often a norm within groups. Even though you may not have planned to send Christmas cards last season, after you began receiving them, you may have changed your mind, at least for those who sent you one first. Reciprocity can be more complex than exchanging gifts or favors.

Salespeople skilled in social influence understand reciprocity, which is why they often first ask for a high amount, one that usually results in an immediate no from the customer. However, before stating the high-end price, they discuss many reasons why the product or service is just what the customer needs. After the cost is stated, and subsequently rejected, a good salesperson will come back with the question, "Would you be interested in buying it if I knocked off 20 percent?" or another appropriate price. This strategy is called a door-in-the-face technique, and the salesperson uses reciprocity discounts to influence the customer's behavior. This strategy is used more often than most people are aware. Some examples are large bills in the tip jar sitting on counters at the coffee shop, in paper cups of panhandlers, or in caps and cases of street musicians. The large bill sets a precedent that it is appropriate to tip in that amount.

Social approval is gained through conformity and obedience. Conformity is the tendency for people to do what others are doing, just because they are doing it. Solomon Asch (1907–1996) conducted a classic experiment where participants included seven actors and one other participant. Each test involved the same ratio of actors to participants. During the experiment, participants were shown cards with three lines printed on them, then asked to state which of the three lines matched a standard line printed on another card. The participant was the last person to be called on, and each of the actors gave the same, but incorrect, answer, creating a group majority. More than half of the participants agreed with the actors and said something they did not believe to be true, the same wrong answer given by the actors. The primary reason honest individuals made false statements was to gain social approval by avoiding going against the group majority. When the majority of the group believes the same truth, conformity ensures that one continues to belong within the group.

Obedience differs from conformity in that people do what someone else tells them to do, just because they were told to do it, and not because others are doing it too. While norms play a role in obedience, the authority status of a person is more influential. People accept that certain figures have the power to both set and enforce rules and punishments.

Imagine a situation in which you are responsible for flipping a switch that administers an electric shock to another person if he or she makes a mistake on a task you are overseeing. In addition, with every mistake made, you must increase the electric voltage, even though you can clearly hear the person scream and beg you to stop, because that is what you were told to do. Stanley Milgram (1933–1984) and colleagues conducted such an experiment exploring the power of authority on obedience behaviors. In this famous experiment, all of the participants were placed in the role of a teacher and were seated at a desk in one room while another researcher playing the part of the learner was strapped into a chair in another room. The teacher's role was to read the word to the learner, and if the learner made a mistake in response, the teacher was to administer progressively increasing electric shocks. Almost all of the teachers became upset and wanted to quit sending the shocks. The authority figure simply restated to the teacher that the experiment required that "you," the teacher, must continue. Eighty percent of the participants in Milgram's study continued to shock the learner even after he screamed, complained, begged, and fell silent. More than 60 percent continued all the way to the highest voltage. Milgram was successful in his goal to demonstrate how ordinary people are capable of doing great and even unspeakable harm to others when ordered to do so.

Destructive obedience behaviors are more common than we might want to believe, and several explanations have been proposed. First, it is believed that authority figures relieve the individual of responsibility for the action by delivering orders. An individual can alleviate any dissonance by justifying that he or she is only carrying out orders. Second, persons of authority have symbols of their authority, such as badges, stripes, hats, and so on. These symbols are reminders that the person bearing them has the right and responsibility to make the rules and administer the punishment. Next, in most settings, the individual only administers a minimal consequence to influence behaviors. If there is resistance, authority figures raise the intensity to influence compliance. Lastly, in most cases, the progression of destructive obedience moves quickly, leaving no time for systematic planning on how to resolve the situation. Orders are often given in reaction to a situation, without time to consider long-term outcomes.

Multiple-Choice Questions

473. One person's control over another's behavior is termed _____.

    (A) approval motive
    (B) social norms
    (C) social influence
    (D) obedience

474. _____ is learning by observing others' actions and consequences.

    (A) Observational learning
    (B) Approval motive
    (C) Social acceptance
    (D) Obedience

475. Receiving recognition from supervisors for hard work done on a project is an example of a _____.

    (A) moral
    (B) reward
    (C) social acceptance
    (D) etiquette

476. The power of one person's reaction to motivate another to act in ways that are appropriate for the situation is known as _____.

    (A) observational learning
    (B) hedonic motive
    (C) altruism
    (D) normative influence

477. The effect on a behavior based on what is considered to be appropriate within a particular group, society, or culture is known as _____.

    (A) normative influence
    (B) approval motive
    (C) social acceptance
    (D) obedience

478. Because humans depend on each other for survival, they will avoid rejection by others as much as possible. Two behaviors that help us gain social approval are

(A) observational learning and door-in-the-face
(B) rewards and punishment
(C) conformity and obedience
(D) social cognition and altruism

479. Solomon Asch's study demonstrating the influence of conformity is an example of which human desire that makes people vulnerable to social influence?

(A) Social acceptance
(B) Self-confidence
(C) Social norms
(D) Hedonic motive

Fill-in-the-Blank Questions

480. _____ is having an impact on how a person thinks, feels, and acts.

481. Three primary desires that make people vulnerable to social influence are _____, _____, and _____.

482. The hedonic principle states a person behaves in a way that produces _____.

483. Albert Bandura conducted a study on childhood aggression and found that children were more likely to behave aggressively if they saw an adult being rewarded for the aggressive behaviors. This is called _____ _____.

484. _____ are customary standards or unwritten rules that provide information about what is appropriate in a social situation.

485. _____ is when we do something because other people are doing it, while _____ is when we do something because a person with authority told us to do it.

486. Stanley Milgram conducted a study in which participants were instructed to administer shock to another person for incorrect answers. The participants did so, even though they did not believe it was the right thing to do. This study demonstrated _____, a type of social influence.

Short-Answer Questions

487. Explain what makes people susceptible to influence.

488. Explain what motivates people to form a line outside of an entrance even though there is no formal instruction to do so.

Cognitive Dissonance Theory

People are more comfortable doing what they believe is right, or maintaining cognitive consonance. Consonance implies that one's actions are in agreement with one's belief and attitude about the information. Attitudes are general evaluations that people have about themselves and the physical and social environment. Emotions, cognitions, and behaviors shape attitudes; however, one attitude can influence another. Cognitive dissonance is common in social situations because the influence of others can motivate us to act in ways we do not agree with. Belonging is essential to social survival, and people will often act in ways that are inconsistent with their attitudes and beliefs.

The theory of cognitive dissonance, developed by Leon Festinger (1919–1989), is based on the idea that people experience discomfort when they act in ways that conflict with their values and beliefs. People experience cognitive dissonance when two or more attitudes conflict. Most people consider themselves to be honest, and value honesty within their relationships. However, many will intentionally lie to another person when the truth is discouraging or painful. For example, if a person believes that telling someone that he or she looks bad will cause hurt feelings, it is unlikely that this person will tell a friend that she looks tired and disheveled. While the belief about the friend's appearance is honest, most people also believe that it is not right to create hurt feelings or self-doubt. Going against one's true belief about a friend's appearance creates discomfort because friendship is typically based on honesty.

Cognitive dissonance is stressful, and the discomfort motivates people toward reducing it either by altering beliefs, incorporating additional information, or downplaying the importance of the dissonant thought. For example, if we believe that our friend's feelings are more important than telling her that we think she looks drained, we justify dishonesty in the friendship. If we know why she is tired, we may add that information to the equation to justify our friend's appearance and believe that our comments are for her benefit.

Festinger proposed three types of dissonance situations that have received the most attention: postdecisional dissonance, effort justification, and insufficient justification. Some decisions are followed by regret, such as a major purchase, and then a second thought about that decision. Postdecisional dissonance results from two conflicting thoughts about two alternatives. The dissonance can be alleviated by undoing the decision, such as returning the purchase, or by reevaluating and adjusting beliefs about the alternative decision so it appears to be clearly the best choice.

Cognitive dissonance also happens when there is a great deal of difficulty involved in following through on the choice made. For example, college students put a great deal of effort toward earning a degree; however, many will stop attending before graduating. Dropping out may be due to lack of financial resources, but many students quit their program due to the continuous demand and difficulty. At one time earning a degree was very important to the student, so why would stopping before graduation be acceptable for some while for others it is not? Effort justification is the reevaluation of the commitment, and deciding if it is worth the effort to earn a degree. Through this evaluation process, the dropout student accepts that the hard work is not worth obtaining the degree, and he or she is more likely going to feel better after not attending college. Whereas a graduating student will accept that obtaining the degree is worth the effort, and this student will not feel better until he or she completes the degree program.

The third situation that can cause cognitive dissonance is justifying an action that is inconsistent with one's attitudes in order to benefit from the situation. In other words, people behave in a way that contradicts a value or belief for a personal gain. For example, celebrities and athletes receive a lot of money for endorsing a product. They will make statements connecting their performance or appearance with the product to promote sales. Although they represent the product, it is unlikely that they believe what they say, nor will their attitude change toward it. They justify doing it because it is a way to earn income and the large benefit removes the dissonance. On the other hand, small benefits do not remove dissonance, such as receiving a very small incentive, or volunteering to support a cause that a person does not believe in. To alleviate the dissonance, people are likely to change attitudes or beliefs in favor of the cause, because little or no incentive is not enough to justify trying to convince others of information that they themselves do not believe to be true.

In general, people are more likely to make modifications when cognitive dissonance effects relationships or social connections. For example, issues related to prejudice and discrimination toward someone close, or within our social network. This is a personal experience and has much to do with why we make situational attributions on our own actions. Take into consideration any one of the social controversies today. Most people know where they stand on abortion, divorce, same-sex marriage, the death penalty, or even homelessness. However, the closer to one's personal life the issue or alternative perspective occurs, the more stress is experienced from cognitive dissonance, and the greater the likelihood of making adjustments to one's beliefs.

Multiple-Choice Questions

489. People experience _____ when they act in ways that conflict with their attitudes and beliefs.

(A) social cognition
(B) negative sense of self
(C) cognitive dissonance
(D) accuracy motive

490. According to the cognitive dissonance theory, people tend to change their _____ to keep them consistent with their _____.

(A) behaviors, attitudes
(B) attitudes, social influence
(C) behaviors, social influence
(D) attitudes, behaviors

491. Which of the following is not one of the three ways in which people experience cognitive dissonance according to Festinger?

(A) postdecisional dissonance
(B) effort justification
(C) social influence
(D) insufficient justification

492. Yesterday while attending an outdoor sporting event, Bill bought a motorcycle so he could go riding with his buddies. Today he is experiencing some remorse and thinks it may have been an impulsive purchase, and he probably won't have time to go riding with his friends. Bill may take the bike back, but he is thinking he could ride the bike to work and save on gas. Which type of cognitive dissonance is Bill experiencing?

(A) Reevaluation justification
(B) Postdecisional dissonance
(C) Effort justification
(D) Insufficient justification

Fill-in-the-Blank Questions

493. The cognitive dissonance theory was developed by _____ to help explain the discomfort people experience in a situation where two or more attitudes or beliefs conflict.

494. The discomfort of cognitive dissonance motivates people toward reducing it either by_____, incorporating additional information, or downplaying the importance of the dissonant thought.

495. Mike has been training for six months to run in an upcoming marathon. He is running for four hours a day and has been able to reach 18 miles. Lately, he is having muscle cramps during the night, and he stiffens up after working all day at his desk job. Mike has always wanted to run a marathon, but he is starting to have second thoughts about the importance of this life goal. He is thinking about changing his registration to the half marathon instead. Mike is experiencing _____ cognitive dissonance.

496. The more _____ is experienced from cognitive dissonance, the greater the likelihood of making adjustments to one's beliefs.

Short-Answer Questions

497. Mark has been a smoker for 15 years. Both of his parents smoke, as do many of his extended family members. A few people have developed health problems such as chronic respiratory diseases, but no one has been diagnosed with cancer yet. Mark's employer has been pushing tobacco cessation programs and has required everyone to attend a company-paid tobacco awareness workshop. Since then Mark has noticed the antismoking billboards around his community and has become a little self-conscious about smoking in public. Mark is experiencing cognitive dissonance. Describe how Mark's cognitive dissonance can be alleviated.

498. Lisa and Kim are best friends. Lately Kim has been emotional due to a breakup with her boyfriend. Lisa knows that Kim complained about her boyfriend all the time, and she wants to tell Kim she feels glad that they have finally broken up. She knows it will upset Kim to hear that, so instead, she tells Kim that she is sorry it happened. Lisa and Kim are always honest with each other, and Lisa is feeling guilty about lying. According to Festinger, what will Lisa do to relieve the cognitive dissonance she is feeling?

499. Stacie recently started a new job that requires her to travel overseas for one year. A few months ago she noticed a mole on her shoulder that has been changing shape, texture, and color. She has seen information on skin cancer and is aware that early detection is critical. Her departure date is in two weeks, and the last thing she wants to deal with is a health problem when her career is taking off, but she is beginning to feel uneasy about putting off going to the doctor until she returns from her work overseas. Explain what Stacie is experiencing.

500. Celebrities and athletes are often recruited to endorse products. They make claims about the products, but they do not believe what they say or even use the product. Explain the role of insufficient justification in this situation.

ANSWERS

Chapter 1 Biological Theories and Perspectives

Nativism, Philosophical Empiricism, and Dualism

1. (D) Psychology is the scientific study of the inner experiences of the mind and the observable actions or behaviors.

2. (A) Origins of psychology are linked to early physiological and philosophical perspectives, dating back to when it was widely accepted that spirits were responsible for health status, bringing good health or illness when they entered the body.

3. (A) Plato believed that knowledge from the previous life somehow makes it into the mind of the new life and therefore, some types of knowledge is innate.

4. (C) Philosophical empiricism is the theory that experiences create knowledge and learning through observation.

5. (C) Plato believed knowledge is innate.

6. (C) Nativism is the idea that knowledge from the previous life somehow makes it into the mind of the new life, and therefore some types of knowledge are innate.

7. (B)

8. philosophers. Ancient philosophers were highly interested in understanding the mind and body connections.

9. At birth, the mind resembles a blank slate.

10. behaviors, mind

11. sensations, reflections. John Locke asserted that knowledge builds from the meanings we give to our sensory experiences and grows as a result of accumulated experiences and ongoing reflection.

12. dualism. Descartes believed that the mind was thought (the mental element), and the body (the physical element) was responsible for generating everything else, including movement and reproduction. He proposed that the mind and body were separate but interacted like a machine.

13. accumulated effect. John Locke asserted that knowledge builds from the meanings we give to our sensory experiences and grows as a result of accumulated experiences and ongoing reflection.

14. nature versus nurture. The nature versus nurture debate questions whether human capabilities are inborn or acquired through experiences. Empiricism states that we learn knowledge through our experiences and interactions; nativists hold that humans are born with innate knowledge and understanding of their reality.

15. Answer should include the following key points: Early Greek philosophers Plato and Aristotle were among the first to explore the question of how the mind works. In seeking to answer this question, philosophers since then have attempted to explain how much knowledge is innate and how much is learned through experience. Current researchers continue to provide pieces to the puzzle by providing evidence that both innate traits and experience affect the mind and shape behaviors.

16. Answer should include the following key points: The study of psychology grew from the ideas and constructs of early philosophers Hippocrates, Socrates, Plato, and Aristotle and their attempts to understand the mind and body. From these early teachings came some of the first constructs of human behavior and some of our first beliefs about physical and mental health. Descartes and Locke promoted a mind-body connection through communication. Descartes saw the mind and body as separate, while Locke proposed that the mind provides reflection on physical experiences, giving meaning and storing the information for later use.

17. Answer should include the following key points: The primary disagreement between empiricism and nativism is whether knowledge is inherited or results from experiences. Empiricism states that we learn knowledge through our experiences and interactions; nativists hold that humans are born with innate knowledge and understanding of their reality. The current nature versus nurture debate continues to explore the significant influence of each and questions the influence of genes against environmental influences. Nature is specific to heredity at conception, while environment is everything that happens after conception. Unlike the debate between empiricism and nativism, the underlying question today is how much influence nature and nurture have on the organism achieving its potential.

18. Answer should include the following key points: Descartes believed in dualism, the idea that the mind and body are distinct from each other but interact and influence each other. In addition, he viewed the body much like a machine, and his theories relied on laws of physics and chemistry. He asserted that the only purpose of the mind was thought (the mental element), and the body (the physical element) was responsible for generating everything else, including movement and reproduction. Descartes was instrumental in demonstrating the stimulus response interactions.

19. Answer should include the following key points: John Locke, an English philosopher, described knowledge attainment as a result of sensations and reflections, or meanings given to sensations. He proposed that reflection immediately follows sensory experiences, and there is an accumulated effect over time. In other words, we give meaning to new sensations by reflecting on earlier experiences. Locke applied this philosophy to explain variances in human perceptions. For example, tangible qualities such as weight and dimension can be consistently measured. On the other hand, complex qualities such as taste, smell, and color experiences are not consistent from one person to the next. Perception of an experience defines the experience in the present, and also works as knowledge for future experiences.

Moreover, people can add bits of their own knowledge to both the tangible and complex qualities of events, making it less likely that perceptions of the same phenomena will be defined in the same way by all people, every time.

Physiology and Psychology

20. (A)

21. (A) Galton was influential in laying a foundation for functionalism in psychology. He held an evolutionary perspective and explored heredity.

22. (C) dualist. The dominant belief at the time was that the mind and body interact but are separate from one another.

23. (D) Paul Broca performed an autopsy on the brain of a deceased patient who had been unable to speak language although he understood it perfectly and found a tumor in the lower left frontal cortex.

24. (C) Gall studied diseased brains of humans and animals that had died, and he made many contributions such as the discovery of white and gray matter.

25. (A)

26. (B)

27. physiology

28. brain

29. reflex

30. phrenology

31. Franz Gall

32. Broca's area

33. Wernicke's area

34. Answer should include the following key points: French physician Paul Broca examined the brain of his deceased patient who had suffered a unique type of language disorder. This patient could understand spoken language, and could use nonverbal gestures to communicate, but was unable to utter a single word. Broca discovered that an area in the frontal lobe of the left hemisphere of the patient's brain was damaged. This area became known as Broca's area. Continued research demonstrated this area to be specific for spoken language functions, as damage to the same area of the right hemisphere does not produce the same outcome. Broca's discovery that specific areas of the brain are connected to specific mental functions provided demonstration that the mind and brain are closely linked. This was significant because at the time, the widely held belief was that the mind is separate but interacts with the brain and body. Researchers continued to demonstrate that the human mind is grounded within the material substance of the brain.

35. Answer should include the following key points: *Phrenology* was temporarily popular as a way to screen employees, assess intelligence in children, and identify many emotional problems in day-to-day life. Developed by Gall, who believed the shape of the brain could provide the evidence to support the theory that different areas of the brain were responsible for particular mental activities, and that the dents and bumps of the skull defined the shape of the brain below it.

36. Answer should include the following key points: Gage's unfortunate accident provided new opportunity to examine how a specific area of the brain affects particular mental activities. Specifically, this was the first case in which scientists could examine the effect of the frontal lobe on emotional regulation, planning, and decision making. Psychology benefited by discovering the important role of the frontal lobe and the subcortical structures below it on human emotional regulation and motivation.

37. Answer should include the following key points: For several years, Broca treated a patient who had been unable to form words and sentences, but could understand everything said to him and could use nonverbal gestures to communicate back. When the patient died, Broca performed an autopsy and found a tumor in the lower left frontal cortex. He made a remarkable discovery of a key area in the brain that is responsible for spoken language. This area is known as *Broca's area*.

38. Answer should include the following key points: Physiologists made it possible for psychology to grow and develop. Early physiologists such as Johannes Müller sparked experimental research and curiosity about the nervous system's function in human behavior. Once experiments on sensory nerves became the focal point, mapping the brain soon followed. Researchers including physicians, physiologists, and biologists quickly discovered that reflexive responses occurred by stimulating particular areas of the brain. Likewise, if an area in the brain or spinal cord was damaged or destroyed, scientists were able to detect subsequent changes in responses, or in some cases, a lack of response. Within a few years, clinical brain research on humans, including autopsies and electrical stimulation, was taking place in hospital settings.

Structuralism and Functionalism

39. (B) William James was instrumental in the functionalist movement, asserting that conscious experiences could not be studied by isolating the elemental qualities.

40. (A)

41. (B)

42. (A)

43. (A)

44. (C)

45. (A)

46. structuralism

47. reaction time

48. introspection

49. each element has a functional role, or a purpose in the experience. The functionalist perspective asserted that conscious experiences could not be studied by isolating the elemental qualities because it distorted the essential flow of consciousness.

50. experimental, introspective observation

51. learned, future. Dewey asserted that behaviors and consciousness cannot be reduced to elements, and that the focus of psychology should be to study the organism as it functions in its environment.

52. survival of the organism in the environment

53. Answer should include the following key points: Structuralism created a way to measure nerve responses in the laboratory setting, where external variables could be controlled to some degree. Sensory thresholds and reaction times were measured, and the conscious experiences of sensory responses were documented as a way to capture the qualitative experience. The qualitative experiences were broken into elemental properties and categorized in an effort to define the relationship between the mind and body quantitatively. Functionalist research focused more on the purpose of the elemental reactions and what each contributes to the experience as a whole. Instead of trying to unify inconsistencies in responses, functionalists recognized that inconsistencies highlight how the experiences influence human behaviors. The qualitative experience for anyone could be attributed to previous sensory processing. Furthermore, humans use knowledge of previous experiences to navigate new experiences and adapt to changes in environmental demands.

54. Answer should include the following key points: Although experimental in nature, categorizing isolated elements of conscious experiences relied on interpretation, which highlighted how inconsistent human experiences can be from one person to the next. In addition, breaking the whole experience into separate sensory responses cannot reliably describe the qualitative human experience. Because introspection is subjective, based on interpretation, it was impossible to use individual elements of human experiences to define conscious experiences as a whole.

55. Answer should include the following key points: Functionalism grew out of structuralism. However, instead of analyzing an element isolated from the other elements associated with the experience; functionalists focused on the role of the element in its relationship, or as it interacts within the experience. Functionalism was influenced by evolution and held that each element of an experience has a functional purpose in promoting the survival of the organism. Functionalism relied on observation methodology of the behavioral adaptations made in response to a stimulus in the natural setting, whereas structuralism relied on experimental methodology of sensory stimuli and threshold response in the lab setting.

56. Answer should include the following key points: Researchers such as Wundt, James, Dewey, and Angell made significant contributions toward establishing psychology as a science and introduced it to the academic setting. Early courses were taught from experimental, structuralist, or functionalist perspectives. Sensory reflexes and conscious experiences helped researchers such as Titchener identify elemental qualities of experiences. Stimulus and reactions to it led to exploration of how the individual adapts behaviors based on outcomes.

57. Answer should include the following key points: William James disagreed with breaking down and isolating elements of conscious experiences for study. He was interested in the functions of the elements, believing that each played an essential role in the experience. In his studies and via inspiration from Darwin's theory of natural selection, James concluded that the conscious elements are adaptive and therefore must be part of the organism's biology. Because people could adapt mental tasks to solve new problems, James proposed that psychology needed to understand the purpose of consciousness and its functions as organisms adapt in their environment.

Evolution

58. **(A)** Evolutionary psychology holds that natural selection is the preservation of mental and behavioral adaptions that ensure survival of the organism and the species.

59. **(D)** Darwin was key in introducing evolution into psychology. He proposed that biological adaptations, the basic principles of natural selection, ensure survival of the species and occasionally create a new species entirely.

60. **(B)** Darwin proposed that biological adaptations ensure survival of the species.

61. **(C)** Darwin proposed that biological adaptations are capable of creating entirely new species, which challenged creationism, the dominant belief that life on earth was created by God.

62. **(A)** Galton founded the science of eugenics, and he believed that mate selection was key to promoting the human race at its greatest potential.

63. **(B)** Attraction from the evolutionary perspective holds that people should naturally be attracted to others who have the genetic tendencies and qualities that will enable offspring to grow, prosper, and become parents themselves and thereby continue survival of the species.

64. **(A)** Galton made significant contributions by applying scientific methodology to quantifying and analyzing psychological elements or traits associated with conscious and unconscious sensations and responses relevant to experiences and the resulting outcome.

65. evolutionary psychology

66. behaviorally

67. adaptations. Adaptations are genetic qualities passed on through heredity that show up in offspring and increase an organism's chance of survival long enough to reproduce.

68. genetic. A genetic trait is an observable trait or behavior that can be linked to a gene.

69. hourglass, triangle. Male body shapes that approximate an inverted triangle and female body shapes that approximate an hourglass are most attractive to the opposite sex.

70. scientific method. Darwin introduced observational methods to study adaptation, and Galton introduced methodology to quantify and analyze psychological elements or traits.

71. Answer should include the following key points: Survival and reproduction are key principles of natural selection and evolution. While in some cases jealousy can be the demise of a relationship, it is also motivating. Feeling jealous inspires a partner to act in ways that reduce the risk of losing a mate. Therefore, people who experience feelings of jealousy are more likely to secure their relationships long enough to produce and raise offspring.

72. Answer should include the following key points: Insights gained from Darwin's theories on adaptation, evolution, and natural selection underlie what we know about how brains work. Psychologists today still believe that the brain and mind are predisposed to adapt to changing environments as they always have, and that adaptability comes from millions of years of heredity. Each generation brings with it the potential to survive the environment of its ancestors; however, environments are always changing, and yet younger generations appear to adapt very well.

73. Answer should include the following key points: Modifications such as changes in food consumption patterns to adapt to availability, or changes in pigment color patterns to blend into a changing environmental color scheme, allowed the organism to live long enough to reproduce and protect its offspring. In addition, these adaptations will begin to show up naturally in offspring through heredity.

74. Answer should include the following key points: Natural selection is the idea that traits that increase chances of successful reproduction will ensure that the species will survive. Humans have a tendency to be attracted to similar features regardless of culture. Male bodies are reported more attractive when they have broad shoulders and a narrowed waist. Females are found to be more attractive when they have an hourglass shape with broad shoulders, small waist, and broad hips. Masculine features in men are associated with higher testosterone and strength, which are desirable traits for producing and providing for offspring. Similarly, youthful feminine features are associated with estrogen, nurturing, and fertility in women and are desirable to men for reproduction. Any physical or behavioral feature that increases the likelihood of reproduction falls within the natural selection perspective.

75. Answer should include the following key points: Evolutionary psychology assumes that human behavior is handed down through millions of years of natural selection. Behaviors that are largely detrimental today such as the stress response, aggression, or preference for high-fat foods were once adaptive in the environment of our ancestors. The stress response promotes survival by preparing us to fight or flee in dangerous situations. Our ancestors were likely to face life-threatening danger regularly; however, most of us rarely do. Yet we continue to activate the stress response, particularly for hypothetical danger (missed deadlines, might be late, etc.). The fight-or-flight response may have saved our ancestors' lives, but today it is linked to several health adversities. For our ancestors, the most aggressive in acquiring food and securing sexual partners were the ones who lived and passed on their genes, while today aggression can lead to negative consequences such as loss of resources and freedom. When food was scarce, our ancestors who had a preference for high-fat foods obtained the calories needed to survive; however, today where food is abundant, high-fat diets can lead to illness and disease.

Chapter 2 Nature versus Nurture: Perspectives on Individual Differences

Genes and Heredity

76. (D) Heredity refers to gene expressions of an observable trait or characteristic. Environmental refers to external influences.

77. (B) Two zygotes originate from the same gametes and thereby share the same or identical DNA.

78. (D) Two zygotes originate from individual gametes and therefore have unique genomes.

79. (A) A recessive gene is present in the genotype, and can be passed on, but it is not expressed in the phenotype because it is paired with a dominant gene.

80. (B) Phenotypes are both and multifactorial, meaning that the interactions of many genes with the many environmental influences before and after the birth of a child can influence observable traits.

81. (C) At conception, the combination of Y and/or X on the twenty-third chromosome determines the gender.

82. polygenetic, multifactorial

83. nature versus nurture debate

84. Human Genome Project

85. 46, 23

86. deoxyribonucleic acid (DNA)

87. genotype

88. heredity

89. phenotype

90. Answer should include the following key points: The genotype is the entire genetic inheritance, while the phenotype is the observable characteristics or traits such as appearance, personality, and intelligence. In many cases, the dominant genetic information will express and be noticeable in the phenotype, while most of the recessive genetic material is carried. However, many traits are polygenic and multifactorial, and the genetic potential may be influenced by environmental factors that hinder or enhance the genotype. For example, nutrition can influence the genetic predisposition on physical development, disease onset, and cognitive development. Therefore, the genotype does not determine the destiny of the phenotype.

91. Answer should include the following key points: When only one allele is necessary for a trait to be expressed in the phenotype, it is considered to be a dominant gene. A dominant gene is more influential in trait expression than a recessive gene, which requires two alleles to express the trait. If a dominant gene is inherited it will be expressed, whereas a recessive gene may be inherited but not expressed in the phenotype.

92. Answer should include the following key points: Brown is the dominant eye color since only one allele is necessary to express it. Therefore, even though parents and grandparents are carriers of the recessive blue eye gene, both parents must pass blue genes to a child in order for the blue eye color to show. In Matt's case, both his mother and his father passed a recessive blue eye allele to him.

93. Answer should include the following key points: Identical twins develop from a single fertilized ovum, and therefore share the exact same genetic material. The two boys have similar strengths that can be attributed to genetics, such as mind-body coordination, critical thinking, physical strength and endurance, and competitiveness. Nurture always influences nature, and while it is possible that an underlying genetic tendency exists for naturally pursuing competitive physical activities, the shared environment actively shaped the development and interest of these boys throughout their childhood. An individual's genes set a person's potential and limitations; however, the environment greatly determines the outcomes of both as a person develops and grows.

94. Answer should include the following key points: Many dominant disorders are fatal in childhood and are not passed on, whereas recessive genes are carried and frequently passed on to offspring. Example: Phenylketonuria (PKU) is a recessive genetic disorder interfering with digestion of protein and if detected early can be treated whereas Tay-Sachs, a recessive genetic enzyme disease, is a fatal childhood disease that cannot be treated even when caught early.

Temperament

95. **(C)** Temperament is a term used to describe and classify emotional behavior traits that include emotional reactivity, self-regulation, and physical activity states.

96. (D) Temperament is inherited (nature); however, environment and experiences (nurture) also have an influence. Some traits may only express under particular situations such as under fear or stress, and actively work to enhance or minimize expression of other traits.

97. (D)

98. (A)

99. (A)

100. (C)

101. (A)

102. nine. There are nine traits used to classify temperaments: activity level, rhythmicity or regularity, approach/withdrawal, adaptability, sensory threshold, intensity, mood, distractibility, and persistence or attention span.

103. New York Longitudinal Study. The New York Longitudinal Study by Alexander Thomas and Stella Chess identified four types of temperament: difficult, easy, slow to warm up, and hard to classify.

104. emotional, behavioral. Temperament patterns tend to be permanent, and over time, emotional and behavioral experiences reinforce how we express them and behavior associated with temperament can be modified over a life span in response to stress and reinforcements.

105. dominant, combination

106. easy

107. emotional and behavioral

108. innate

109. Approach/withdrawal, adaptability, and rhythmicity. Each trait is rated on a scale along a spectrum with high and low polar opposites. Approach/withdrawal refers to the immediate reaction to a new experience: acceptance or rejection. Adaptability refers to how soon after a withdrawal/rejection occurrence a person begins to adapt to the new situation. Rhythmicity refers to regularity (internal) in sleep-wake cycles and frequency of hunger.

110. Answer should include the following key points: Approach/withdrawal refers to the immediate reaction to a new experience: acceptance or rejection. Ann and Jason rate difficult because they are struggling to accept the new situation. Ann is spending less time with Jason because she is returning to her job, and Ann is rejecting Jason's resulting irregular feeding and sleeping patterns, and this resistance is causing a decrease in desire and frequency of positive attention and playful bonding behaviors. Jason has not been able to accept his mother's new schedule or her lack of attention and affection during interactions.

Adaptability refers to how soon after a withdrawal/rejection occurrence a person begins to adapt to the new situation. Ann and Jason rate difficult because they were not able to adjust to the new situation in a short period of time. Three months is considered more than a moderate period of time to adapt to a new change. Neither Jason nor Ann has made any improvements in adapting to the change over this time, which suggests that they need still more time to adjust to the change.

Rhythmicity refers to regularity (internal) in sleep-wake cycles and frequency of hunger. Ann and Jason rate difficult because both are experiencing low regularity for sleeping and for being hungry at the time their schedule deems appropriate. Jason is no longer sleeping for more than a few hours during the night, and Ann's sleep is irregular even on Mark's turn to care for Jason during the night. Ann has no appetite to eat at mealtime and appears to be combating fatigue with sugar. Jason is taking longer to eat; nor is he drinking his entire bottle.

111. activity level: difficult; persistence and attention span: difficult. Activity level refers to the frequency and speed of movement; persistence and attention span refer to the length of uninterrupted attention to a single activity and spontaneous return to a task after interruption.

Each trait is rated on a scale along a spectrum with high and low polar opposites. Mark is high on activity and low on persistence and attention span. High on activity is classified as difficult, and low on persistence and attention span is also classified as difficult. Both of these require more effort from parents, teachers, and other caregivers in regard to task completion and level of supervision required.

112. mood: difficult; threshold: difficult. Mood refers to the predominance of either a positive or negative versus a neutral mood expression. Threshold refers to the minimum strength of a stimulus required to cause a child to react or attend. Lexie responds with discontent quickly to the smallest change in sensory stimuli, temperature, touch, and sound. She is more often discontent, and once she is upset she does not return to a neutral mood quickly.

113. persistence and attention span: easy; distractibility: easy. Persistence and attention span refer to the length of uninterrupted attention to a single activity, and spontaneous return to a task after interruption. Distractibility refers to ease with which attention can be drawn away from an ongoing activity by a new stimulus. Tyler is able to resist letting the behaviors of the child seated next to him get in the way of him finishing his class assignment. His ability to ignore distractions allows him to complete his work with minimal errors.

Personality

114. (B)

115. (C)

116. (A)

117. (A)

118. (C)

119. (C)

120. (D) OCEAN is the acronym for the Big Five personality factors.

121. negatively

122. traits

123. past, present, and future

124. bipolar

125. maladaptive

126. neurotransmitter

127. The Rorschach Inkblot Test and the Thematic Apperception Test

128. Answer should include the following key points: Eysenck believed that personality was biologically based, and how strongly the trait is expressed depends on heritability, with the exception of neurotic behaviors, which to Eysenck are learned.

129. Answer should include the following key points: Personality is genetically based and evident in early childhood but is influenced by environmental factors. Personality traits remain mostly consistent, but life events can alter the degree of expression intensities.

130. Answer should include the following key points: Trait theories suggest that everyone has certain personality traits, but the degree that the trait is expressed differs from one person to the next. People tend to have traits that are dominant, noticeable all of the time even if the degree fluctuates.

131. Answer should include the following key points: Personality can be defined by observing the way people achieve their goals, and delay self-gratification in order to avoid a negative consequence. During the successful moments, people are confident, happy, optimistic, and motivated, but as they grow closer to their potential, they begin to be unhappy, unmotivated, and less confident and optimist about reaching the goal. In addition, postponement of something desired, or delaying gratification, triggers a physiological stress response causing discomfort and anxiety. Ongoing stressors have a negative effect on personality. Catell suggested that personality is a series of behaviors that fall between two extremes on 16 source traits, while Eysenck proposed that behaviors indicate degrees of three personality factors.

132. Answer should include the following key points: Neurotransmitters (chemicals) dopamine, serotonin, and norepinephrine are associated with behavioral activation, inhibition, and regulation, memory, mood, motivation, attention, eating, and sleeping behaviors. Neurotransmitters play a role in temperament and are linked to the five personality traits.

Imbalances in production, regulation, release, and uptake of any one of the neurochemicals can result in a difficult temperament and negative personality expression. Maladaptive behaviors, antisocial behaviors, and inflexibility are indicative of personality disorders and are diagnosed when it becomes difficult for a person to function in expected social roles.

133. Answer should include the following key points: The MMPI-2 is used to assess for personality disorders in a clinical setting. Through a series of questions, the test finds patterns that may indicate abnormal personality traits indicative of a psychological disorder. It is a psychological tool administered and interpreted by qualified mental health professionals.

Environment
134. (A) Heredity refers to gene expressions of an observable trait or characteristic. Environmental refers to external influences.

135. (B) A critical period is a time during embryonic development at which specific kinds of growth must take place if the embryo is to develop normally.

136. (D) Age of viability refers to the point in development in which the brain has matured to allow a fetus to survive if born prematurely.

137. (A) Teratogens are external influences that have a negative influence on prenatal development such as drugs, chemicals, viruses, or other external factors that cause birth defects.

138. (D) Urie Bronfenbrenner (1917–2005) proposed ecological models to identify levels of social support surrounding an individual, and the dynamic interactions between the systems.

139. (C) Microsystem includes those within the immediate surroundings, such as family and friends; exosystem consists of the various institutions in which the individual interacts such as churches, schools, and work; macrosystem includes the cultural values, economic policies, and political processes; chronosystem consists of the historical content and context; and mesosystem includes the dynamic interactions between the first three support systems.

140. (C) Microsystem includes those within the immediate surroundings, such as family and friends; exosystem consists of the various institutions in which the individual interacts such as churches, schools, and work.

141. germinal, embryonic, fetal. The germinal period is from conception through the first two weeks, embryonic lasts from the third week through the eighth week, and the fetal period begins on the ninth week and ends at birth.

142. having adequate brain development

143. environment. The environment, which includes all external influences, plays a key role in achieving genetic potential.

144. teratogens. Teratogens are agents that can cross the placenta and interfere with normal development. These agents are transmitted to the developing embryo or fetus via the mother and can include virus, nutrition, drugs (prescription, over the counter, and recreational), alcohol, chemicals, and air pollutants.

145. psychosocial. The psychosocial environment includes parents, members within the community, culture, additional family members, and friends.

146. **(C)** chronosystem. Chronosystem consists of the historical content and context.

147. **(C)** dysfunctional. A functional family provides basic necessities, promotes learning, fosters self-respect, cultivates friendships, and promotes stability and harmony.

148. Answer should include the following key points: Environmental influences on fetal development include the mother's nutrition and health. Teratogen exposure such as drugs, alcohol, tobacco, poor air quality, and other chemical exposure during a critical period can have a negative influence on prenatal development.

149. Answer should include the following key points: A critical period is a time when specific kinds of growth must take place if the embryo is going to develop normally. Pregnancy lasts for about 38 weeks and is broken down into three main periods of development. The germinal period lasts for the first two weeks, during which time there is rapid cell division and the early beginnings of cell differentiation. The third week through the eighth week is the embryonic period, a critical period for body structures development. The fetal period begins at the ninth week and lasts until birth. During this time sex organs develop and body systems begin functioning. At 22 weeks, the brain is developed to a point that a preterm infant could survive; however, each day after this age of viability, the chances of survival increase significantly. Teratogen exposure at any point during these three periods can result in a physical, cognitive, or behavioral abnormality. Importantly, many teratogens have a threshold effect and may not interfere with development unless the threshold is reached.

150. Answer should include the following key points: The first level, microsystem, includes those within the immediate surroundings, such as family and friends. The second level, the exosystem, consists of the various institutions in which the individual interacts, such as churches, schools, and work settings. The third level, macrosystem, includes the cultural values, economic policies, and political processes. Each system is connected to the others and provides resources and vulnerabilities causing instability for an individual.

151. Answer should include the following key points: Patterns of transitions and opportunities over the course of one's life influence stability and well-being. Development of vaccinations, abundance of resources, famine, war, medical advances, and policy changes have lasting effects on people with the same cohort, or age group.

152. Answer should include the following key points: The structure of a family is less important than how the family functions on childhood resilience. Family functioning is measured by how well the family provides the necessities, promotes learning, fosters self-respect, cultivates friendships, and promotes harmony. Three factors that increase the likelihood of a family to become dysfunctional are low income, low stability, and low harmony. Family structure tends to influence family function by way of resource availability. A nuclear family (with two biological or adoptive parents) can provide the greatest financial and biopsychosocial resources. Single-parent homes tend to have fewer biopsychosocial resources necessary for a stable environment. Single parents often rely on resources from one source and are more likely to fall into low-income categories. Regardless of the structure, families that do not support all of their members are considered dysfunctional.

153. Answer should include the following key points: Socioeconomic status (SES) refers to income, wealth, occupation, education, and place of residence. SES is protective when the resources available adequately meet the needs of the family. Higher income and education correlate with better health and more health resources. Low SES presents disadvantages, limits opportunities, and can negatively affect biopsychosocial development at every age, and money problems are the primary source of stress and family conflict and instability. Low SES negatively affects the very young and very old more; however, low income is associated with physical and mental health problems and higher stress, substance abuse, and obesity rates. Furthermore, financial resources influence healthcare resources, and low-income homes tend to have fewer options in regard to healthcare services. Opportunities for education and social engagement may be limited or inaccessible due to lack of funding and demographic location. Often school-based and community social activities require a fee to participate or may not be easily accessible. For many people, participation in social activities influences sense of within and without group belonging. People tend to desire social norms and are influenced by what others are doing. Normative influence has a powerful effect on decisions and behaviors, and on social status within cultural contexts.

154. Answer should include the following key points: The peer culture provides an essential environment for developing self-concept, self-esteem, and identity. With age, friendships become increasingly more influential in achieving a sense of belonging. Friendships are based on qualities such as trustworthiness, cooperation, fairness, and kindness and become the most important relationships as early as middle childhood. Close friendships provide acceptance, approval, and support beginning in adolescence. Adult support networks are vast and exist in natural settings such as friendly encounters with members in the community or work colleagues; however, close friendships continue to be among the most important relationships.

Parenting
155. (D)

156. (C)

157. (A)

158. (D)

159. (C)

160. (B)

161. (A)

162. environmental

163. Strange Situation

164. easily comforted

165. predictable

166. reinforce. Attachment is set in early childhood, but it is vulnerable to experiences across the life span. Often people act in ways that lead to expected outcomes; and behaviors associated with each attachment style produce expected outcomes most of the time.

167. expression of warmth, strategies for discipline, communication, and expectations for maturity

168. permissive

169. Answer should include the following key points: The strength of this bond is evident in children by the child's first birthday by how the child seeks proximity, or works to be near the parent, and in how comforted a child is when the parent returns from being away. Infants with secure attachments overcome separation anxiety in a timely manner and feel confident to explore and learn about the surrounding environment.

170. Answer should include the following key points: In this procedure, the mother and child begin in the same strange setting in which there are a variety of toys for the child to play with. In three-minute intervals, the mother leaves, and then returns. Another variation of this experiment may include the addition of a stranger. Researchers measure the child's desire and effort to seek proximity with the mother and the degree of distress experienced when she is out of sight. They observe how easily comforted the child is by the mother, and how soon the child resumes playing upon her return.

171. Answer should include the following key points: Secure attachments: child desires and seeks proximity with the mother and experiences some distress when she is out of sight. Upon her return, securely attached infants are comforted by the mother and tend to resume playing soon after.

Insecurely attached infants are not easily comforted upon reuniting with the mother. Infants with avoidant attachments do not seem to mind when the mother leaves their sight and will not usually seek proximity when she returns. It seems as if these infants do not have an emotional need for the mother. Infants with resistant/ambivalent attachments are bothered by separation from the mother, however her return does not provide them the comfort that it does for a securely attached child. This child is likely to be both angry with the mother and in need of her closeness.

The manner in which children with a disorganized attachment pattern respond is unpredictable. The defining characteristic of this type of attachment is that the child may seek proximity through avoidance behaviors, or in ways that are contradictory to being close to the parent.

172. Answer should include the following key points: Avoidant types of attachment occur when the parent consistently does not respond to the infant's distress or crying. The more distal the parenting approach, the more the infant learns to self-calm, and therefore is more likely to develop an avoidant attachment. These attachment behaviors tend to result from inconsistencies in the parent's response to the infant's distress. The parent may at times be prompt and comforting, while at other times, neglectful.

Children with disorganized or insecure attachments adapt differently to caregiver and environmental changes or inconsistencies. A child with an avoidant attachment pattern might just as easily be comforted by someone other than the parent, even if it is a stranger. As they age, these children are more likely to exhibit externalizing coping behaviors when distressed. On the other hand, children with resistant/ambivalent attachment patterns experience much more anxiety and inability to cope with separation, and they are not easily comforted by others. They are also more likely to internalize feelings when coping with stress. Those with disorganized attachments tend to have more aggression and hostility in social interactions, and there is a strong correlation to pathology. Attachment remains stable through adolescence and plays a key role in coping and adjusting to significant changes and loss. Many researchers believe that if a secure attachment is not formed by age two, it is not likely to happen. Insecure attachments leave a child vulnerable to adjusting and therefore less resilient. They are also more likely to have difficulties in adult relationships due to these early working models.

173. Answer should include the following key points: Securely attached adults are able to balance interdependence and independence in relationships. They view themselves and others positively and hold a set of working models for healthy relationship behaviors and expectations. Anxious-preoccupied attachment behaviors include suspicions and worry and an underlying expectation for negative outcomes, and adults often act impulsively on their suspicions and worry. Adults with a dismissive-avoidant attachment style have a strong preference for independence and alone time, and they are more likely to view relationships as not worth the inevitable painful outcome. They believe they are self-sufficient and do not need close companionships. Adults with a fearful-avoidant attachment style often engage in contradictory behaviors. They want a close relationship but are anxious in relationships because they lack trust in their partner, or feel distressed and uncertain. Often these adults have a low self-worth, and they usually internalize their feelings.

174. Answer should include the following key points: Communication is low, and primarily parent-to-child, and there is an expectation that the child will do what the parent says, because the parent says. Authoritarian parents love their children and expect them to do their best, but usually "best" is defined by the parent. Emotions are rarely expressed except for anger or disappointment when the child makes a mistake, and mistakes are often punished. Children are generally obedient when they are young and fear the parents' disapproval or punishment. Adolescents tend to internalize emotions and be overly self-critical, or they may become rebellious and leave home as soon as they are able to. Overall, children of authoritarian parents report low levels of happiness and have inadequate social competence and low self-esteem. Authoritarian parenting styles often create unhappy, poorly accepted, and resentful young people who struggle to function in the social contexts essential for performing adult roles.

175. Answer should include the following key points: Authoritative parents are highly affectionate; they have high communication between parent and child, instead of from one or the other. Parents with an authoritative style set expectations for maturity and discipline based on each child's developmental abilities. This may seem inconsistent among children within the same family unit; however, due to the high level of communication and expression of warmth, children gain a high level of autonomy. As a result, children develop adequate self-esteem and social competence, and they report higher happiness. They tend to do better in school, are well liked by others, and therefore are more successful in transitioning to adulthood roles.

Chapter 3 Stages of Psychosocial Development

Psychosexual Stages of Development

176. (C)

177. (D)

178. (A)

179. (B)

180. (C)

181. (B)

182. (C) Freud was among the first to show that early childhood experiences, in particular parent-child interactions, have an effect on adult psychosocial development.

183. psychoanalytical theory

184. unconsciously

185. psychosexual stages

186. id, ego, superego

187. conflict

188. Oedipus complex

189. phallic

190. Answer should include the following key points: The oral stage, birth through the first year, is characterized by the infant's energy channeled toward satisfying needs through the mouth. Sucking, crying, and cooing are important behaviors during this time of life. In the anal stage (ages one to three), in which control over the body becomes the source of pleasure as the anal sphincter develops, the child learns that he or she can control holding and releasing. The phallic stage (ages three through five) is characterized by focus primarily on the genital region. Children experience pleasurable sensations from fondling the genitals, and sexual drives are often directed as crushes toward the opposite-sex parent. In the latency stage (age six to puberty), psychosexual urges are quiet. The id, ego, and superego continue to refine personality, though children are busy adopting roles and learning relevant skills. In the genital stage, which lasts through adulthood, the ego works to keep the id and superego in balance as the teenager and emerging adult pursues intimacy and assumes adult roles.

191. Answer should include the following key points: Oral stage: Parent-child conflict centers around feeding and weaning; personality traits associated with an oral fixated personality include excessive talking, overeating, chain smoking, crying easily; being dependent, addictive, or needy; or having overwhelming feelings of helplessness.

Anal stage: Parent-child conflict centers on toilet training; personality traits associated with an anal fixated personality include being extremely orderly or sloppy, controlling or disorganized.

Phallic stage: Parent-child conflict centers on the Oedipus or Electra complex—competing and identifying with the same-sex parent. Personality traits associated with a phallic fixated personality include being extremely flirty, vain, jealous, or competitive or strongly internalized prohibitions against sexual behavior or against asserting oneself in intimate relationships.

Latency stage: This stage has no fixated personality traits. Psychosexual urges are quiet as the id, ego, and superego continue to refine personality and children adopt roles and learn relevant skills.

Genital stage: Parent-child conflicts center around adult responsibilities. Personality traits associated with the genital stage include commitment and investment into work and love, and capacity for healthy relationships. Genital stage fixations tend to be sexual impulses and behaviors.

192. Answer should include the following key points: The biological self (id) is active at birth, and its purpose is to ensure survival. Throughout childhood the id is self-serving and driven toward pleasure, satisfaction, and gratification. As a child learns that acting on instinct and self-interest is not always appropriate, the rational self (ego) develops. The child begins to coordinate socially appropriate behaviors with goal attainment and self-gratification. Children become better at considering the consequences of actions in decision making. In addition, the child begins to incorporate parental values and morals into decision making (superego), the source of conflict between the pleasure of gratification and the guilt of doing something parents disapproved of. The ego works to satisfy both the wants of the id and the morals of the superego.

193. Answer should include the following key points: While Freud's theory emphasized the important role of the parent-child relationship, it has been criticized for being too focused on unconscious drives and minimizes the role of individual conscious control. It was considered controversial due to an emphasis on sexual experiences and desires.

194. Answer should include the following key points: Freud considered adolescence as the final age for development. He believed children enter into a period of latency in which psychosexual urges are quiet. The id, ego, and superego continue to refine personality, though children are busy adopting roles and learning relevant skills. This period of calm ends with the onset of puberty, when children move into the genital stage, the final stage lasting through adulthood. In late adolescence and adulthood, ego works to keep id and superego in balance as freedoms to pursue intimacy increase. Because fulfilling responsible adult roles is important, the young adult can resist sexual impulsive gratifications to engage in work, pursue higher education, and potentially start a family.

195. Answer should include the following key points: Around age two when the child is in the anal stage, Freud considered the potty training years to be a source of conflict because the child has learned he or she can have control over elimination activities while at the same time the parent is attempting to force control and to manage them. The id, driven toward pleasure, satisfaction, and gratification, and the ego, striving to seek approval for acting in appropriate ways, are both active.

196. Answer should include the following key points: He presented the idea that behaviors are unconsciously driven and not the results of rational choices. Freud's theory was largely based on his clinical treatments of patients with hysteria. He discovered that most of his patients' problems were linked to effects of earlier childhood experiences, many of which could not be remembered. Each stage has a potential conflict, and how the child experiences and resolves the conflict, especially during the first three stages, determines personality patterns throughout life. Freud asserted that a crisis can occur at any stage and may lead to a fixation in personality.

Psychosocial Stages of Development

197. (B)

198. (B)

199. (A)

200. (B)

201. (B)

202. (A)

203. (D)

204. guilt

205. identity

206. Generativity versus stagnation

207. despair

208. more

209. vocational, gender, religion, and political

210. self-concept

211. Answer should include the following key points: After age two, young children become aware of what they are capable of and what they are not. When their tasks match their abilities, children feel a sense of pride; however, if they perform below what they believe themselves capable of, they feel shame. Pride develops from within children from positive perceptions of themselves and their performance. However, shame comes from a child's awareness of the parent's disapproval and negative parental criticism. While a parent's praise will not cause the child to feel pride, remaining emotionally neutral when providing feedback on the child's behavior creates a safe space for the child to continue to do things on his or her own.

212. Answer should include the following key points: Erickson's stage crisis is overcoming the industry versus inferiority crisis of stage 4. Once children enter into school systems, learning becomes a primary task. Between ages 6 and 12, a child's attention is focused on achievement, and self-concept and self-esteem correlate with what one can do and how well it can be done. Knowledge and application are central to how one feels about oneself. The positive personality virtue is competence, and the negative outcome is a lack of competence. While caregiver response is still impactful, others outside the family are important as well. Social comparison provides a judgment basis of being the best, good, or the worst at a particular task. Peer culture provides a value system for winning and losing and being first or last. Children strive to find a comfortable balance in order to be accepted in social contexts.

213. Answer should include the following key points: Self-understanding achieved in the previous stage ensures that young adults are secure enough about their identity that they can tolerate differences in others to find love in relationships. Intimate relationships of all types provide biopsychosocial satisfaction and demand efforts of the individual, often in the form of sacrificing something of the self. For many, marriage is a primary benchmark in early adulthood, and children often follow marriage. Lack of fidelity increases self-protective behaviors, which can lead to isolation, and isolating to avoid negative aspects of social commitments can instill a fear of intimacy.

214. Answer should include the following key points: Freud and Erikson both believed adulthood echoed childhood experiences. Freud proposed five stages and suggested that development ended at adolescence, while Erikson proposed eight stages and believed that human development is lifelong. Erickson, like Freud, believed that the caregiver's response to meeting an infant's needs in the first year was important. Erikson believed that the child would learn how reliable the world around him or her is based on the caregiver's sensitivity. Freud oriented toward the dark side of human behavior, suggesting that fixated personalities could only be fixed through psychoanalysis, whereas Erikson highlighted the relevance of social supports and culture and suggested that an unresolved crisis can be resolved in a later stage. Erickson also believed that identity is not fixed upon transitioning from adolescence into adulthood, and circumstances may lead a person to enter into a particular adult stage at any time.

215. Answer should include the following key points: Identity achievement, in which an individual understands who he or she is as a unique individual, is characterized by high exploration and high commitment. Identity diffusion, in which an individual is apathetic about who he or she is, is characterized by no exploration and no commitment. Identity moratorium, in which an individual is delaying a decision about identity formation to explore alternatives, is characterized by high exploration and low commitment. Identity foreclosure, in which premature identity formation adopts parents' or society's roles and values, is characterized by no exploration and high commitment.

216. Answer should include the following key points: According to Erikson, adolescents and emerging adults may choose an identity moratorium and explore other roles, though temporary, before making a decision about their career. College provides an avenue for exploration in which an individual can pursue interests and career simultaneously. Additionally, college, missions, Peace Corps, and internships allow adolescents and young adults the freedom to explore different career areas without a lifelong commitment.

217. Answer should include the following key points: Erikson indicated that the adult stages are not one directional and that adults can cycle through them. However, he does stress that healthy development at previous stages promotes successful crisis resolution in the next. Erikson felt that success in achieving generativity prevented disparity in later adulthood. Self-concept during later adult years is associated with cognitive abilities, physical appearance, relationships, health, and life satisfaction. The eighth stage, integrity versus despair, is when adults must face limitations and overcome prejudices associated with limitations, while still contributing to the well-being of humanity. At the same time, death and loss become a significant part of life for the older adult as familiar people pass away and bring about the reality of one's own mortality. Regret and fear of dying are thought to be indications of despair brought on by accumulated conflicts that have not been resolved. Therefore, remaining connected to one's culture, society, and family helps the older adult maintain a degree of competence and adequacy necessary to support a healthy identity.

Maslow's Hierarchy of Needs

218. (B)

219. (D) Socioeconomic status is a measure of demographics; everyone falls within a socioeconomic status. Self-sufficiency, committed relationship, and nourishment are goals to be attained in progressing toward self-actualization.

220. (D)

221. (B)

222. (A)

223. (B)

224. (B)

225. self-actualization

226. humanistic

227. basic needs, or deficit needs. Maslow proposed a hierarchical model that emphasized positive intentions driven by need fulfillment. In order to reach potential, each level related to survival must be obtained beginning with food, water, sleep, shelter, intimacy, and status.

228. security and confidence

229. peak experience

230. older, younger

231. secure, confident

232. 1. Physiological: needing food, water, warmth, and air; 2. Safety: feeling protected from injury and death; 3.Love and belonging: having loving friends, family, and community; 4. Esteem: being respected by the wider community as well as by oneself; 5. Self-actualization: becoming truly oneself, fulfilling one's unique potential.

233. Answer should include the following key points: The order of the hierarchy is important because the needs at each level are the motivators. Maslow believed humans are motivated to grow and develop interpersonally, and as basic needs are met, motivation for personal growth follows. The first level includes physiological needs of food, sleep, and sex. When physiological needs are met, people are motivated to acquire safety and security (level two), such as social order, work, and a sense of stability. The third level is love and belonging, to feel satisfied and safe in a committed relationship. When people have met physiological, safety, and belonging needs, they become motivated to advance esteem from self and others. Esteem is the first higher level, where the motivation is directed toward increasing a value rather than filling a deficit. Self-sufficiency and competency are key to providing a rich, fulfilled, and effortless sense of esteem. Having achieved esteem, individuals begin to acquire high degrees of acceptance of themselves, others, and events; however, with an understanding of truth, not giving in. By accepting the truth, one can begin to see the path to resolution or goal attainment. It is this clarity that Maslow thought separated the self-actualized from others by the way they approach fulfilling needs. Needs can be met through positive or negative behaviors; however, self-actualization and happiness can only be acquired through personal growth and self-understanding.

234. Answer should include the following key points: Maslow's theory focuses on the positive aspects of humans and personal development, whereas Freud focused on the selfish darker side of human personality as people gratify needs, and Erikson focused on the importance of interpersonal relationships on development of the self. Maslow studied highly achieved individuals, and Freud studied people in treatment. Maslow, Freud, and Erikson emphasized the influence of parental love during the first two years of life and the effect it can have on the adult self. Erikson and Maslow believed that failure to achieve satisfaction or balance at previous stages can influence efforts and success at the next.

235. Answer should include the following key points: Maslow believed humans are motivated to grow and develop personally, and as basic needs are met, motivation for personal growth follows. The first level includes physiological needs of food, sleep, and sex. Mark is employed, earning income, and in an intimate relationship. When physiological needs are met, people are motivated to acquire safety and security (level two), such as social order, work, and a sense of stability. With Mark's promotion, he's feeling stable in his income resources and considering buying a home. The third level is love and belonging, to feel satisfied and safe in a committed relationship. Mark has been involved with Shelly for a length of time, and now that he has stable income he is ready to take the relationship to the next level and ask her to marry him.

236. Answer should include the following key points: Self-actualized individuals tend to maintain objectivity, have great acceptance of themselves and others, are committed and dedicated to their work or ambitions, and are creative thinkers. Self-actualized individuals are self-sufficient, competent, have a need for independence, and resist conforming. They have a strong need to benefit humanity. Maslow declared that self-actualized persons have peak experiences, or moments of profound love, understanding, and happiness in which there is a sense of complete harmony, oneness, or goodness.

Chapter 4 Behavioral Theories and Perspectives

Animal Psychology: Stimulus and Response Learning

237. (B)

238. (A)

239. (B)

240. (A)

241. (C) cognition

242. (B)

243. (D) Watson believed that emotions were physiological responses to specific stimuli that could be learned through conditioning.

244. learning theory

245. animal

246. objective methodology

247. instrumental behavior

248. conditioned learning and reinforcement

249. objective and measurable

250. learned response

251. Answer should include the following key points: The cats in Thorndike's experiments manipulated objects in their environment in order to get to food. The cats learned to escape the puzzle box through a series of trial-and-error behaviors. Initially the cats pawed through the crate bars to try to get to the food, then inside the crate to find an opening. The first successful pressing of the lever was by accident, but in repeated attempts the cats progressively stopped behaviors that did not result in the door opening. In each attempt, the cat's pawing behaviors remained closer to the latch area until it discovered only the specific behavior, pressing the lever, that was needed.

252. Answer should include the following key points: Established by Thorndike, the law of effect proposes that actions are associated with situations. Acts that produce satisfaction in a given situation become associated with that situation, and reinforcement makes it likely the action will recur. Examples can be anything that demonstrates one or more actions that result in goal attainment.

253. Answer should include the following key points: Thorndike believed that learning was a series of connections between objectively verifiable situations and responses, or associations. Any behavior that happens in a particular situation becomes associated with the situation. For example, the cat stuck in the box (situation) begins pawing (behavior) and accidently touches the latch to eventually open the door (satisfaction).

254. Answer should include the following key points: The more often a behavior or response occurs in a given situation, the greater the association. In other words, the more a goal-directed behavior is performed, the more likely the behavior will happen when presented with the goal. Example: Each time the cat is in the box it paws in the same area that it pawed previously when the door opened.

255. Answer should include the following key points: Hans appeared to have human cognitive abilities, which could not be attributed to any type of fraud by Hans's owner. Using an experimental method consisting of a control group and an experimental group, a grad student was able to demonstrate that Hans was truly smart, but not because he could do math or spell. The control group would ask Hans questions, but they did not know the answers, whereas the experimental group would ask Hans questions and knew the answers. Hans answered almost every question asked by the experimental group, but none asked by the control group. This experiment demonstrated that Hans had learned to detect subtle cues for his correct answers, and he was rewarded for doing so.

256. Answer should include the following key points: Watson believed that mental processes could not be studied scientifically because they were subjective. He believed that if psychology was to be a science, it should confine its subject matter to objectively observable behavior. Watson's research included explaining instinct, emotion, and thoughts using objective stimulus-response terms. Instincts, according to Watson, were socially conditioned responses, and any traits or talents that one was born with could be overridden through learning. Watson believed that emotions were physiological responses to specific stimuli. The internal physical reactions are accompanied by a learned overt response that is physically observable. Watson proposed that emotions could be conditioned to stimuli that would otherwise not be able to elicit them.

257. Answer should include the following key points: Albert initially exhibited no prior fears to these objects. Watson and colleagues conducted research examining these fear reflexes. In order to demonstrate that emotional reactions are conditioned, they associated an unrelated stimulus, the white rat, with a loud clanking noise. Prior to the experiment, the white rat was a neutral stimulus to the infant. The loud noise was an unconditioned stimulus (US) naturally triggering fear, an unconditioned response (UR). During the experiment, the neutral stimulus was paired with the US, which created the association and led to a conditioned emotional response (CER). After several pairings, Albert began to exhibit fear when presented with the white rat without the loud noise. The white rat had now become a conditioned stimulus (CS), and his fear of it was a conditioned response (CR). Watson and colleagues demonstrated that emotional reactions, in this case fear, are conditioned.

Classical Conditioning

258. (B)

259. (A)

260. (C)

261. (C)

262. (C)

263. (A)

264. (A)

265. Ivan Pavlov

266. associated or connected

267. behaviorist

268. reinforced

269. extinction

270. classical conditioning

271. conditioned stimulus

272. conditioned response

273. Answer should include the following key points: Upon realization that his dogs had learned cues leading to the food presentation, Pavlov declared animals and humans had respondent reflexes and that respondent conditioning, or learning, occurs when a particular response becomes linked to a particular stimulus.

274. Answer should include the following key points: Unconditioned stimulus (UCS)—a stimulus that automatically brings about a particular response without having been learned, typically a reflex. Unconditioned response (UCR)—a response originally given to an unconditioned stimulus; it is natural and requires no association or training. Conditioned stimulus (CS)—a stimulus that was originally neutral but through pairing has become associated with the unconditioned stimulus to bring about a conditioned response. Conditioned response (CR)—a learned or acquired response to a previously neutral stimulus.

275. Answer should include the following key points: During the acquisition phase, a neutral stimulus is paired with an unconditioned stimulus (UCS) repeatedly to form an association. The goal of acquisition is to learn to associate the neutral stimulus with the UCS until the neutral stimulus becomes a conditioned stimulus (CS). In other words, when the neutral stimulus no longer needs to be paired with the UCS to bring about the desired response.

276. Answer should include the following key points: The extinction process involves removal of the reinforcement that the organism has previously learned to predict to follow the conditioned stimuli. When a reinforcement does not follow repeatedly, the acquired behaviors quickly diminish and steadily decrease until they no longer occur.

277. unconditioned stimulus, unconditioned response. One child crying because another child hits her does not require learning—it is a natural response.

278. conditioned stimulus. Mindy has associated the day care with the child hitting her.

279. conditioned response. Mindy cries because she has involuntarily learned that day care means being hurt.

280. Removal of the child hitting Mindy for an extended amount of time

Operant Conditioning

281. (D)

282. (A)

283. (A)

284. (B)

285. (C)

286. (B)

287. (C)

288. operant

289. triggered

290. reduces a biological need. Thorndike advocated for the role of the organism in taking actions to achieve a goal, stating that outcomes of behaviors do more than satisfy needs and drives. Outcomes work to establish a relationship between the organism and its environment.

291. conscious, outcomes

292. organism's enjoyment

293. Behavior modification

294. continuous short

295. Answer should include the following key points: Pavlov is associated with classical conditioning. Classical conditioning is a process by which a person learns to associate a neutral stimulus with a meaningful stimulus, gradually reacting to the neutral stimulus with the same behavior as the meaningful one. Classical conditioning is involuntary learning; operant conditioning is voluntary learning. Skinner is associated with operant conditioning. In operant conditioning a person performs some action and then a response occurs. If the response is pleasurable, the person is likely to repeat the action. If the response is unpleasant, the person is unlikely to repeat the action.

296. Answer should include the following key points: Skinner's theory of operant conditioning is that behaviors are largely due to genetic endowment and environmental reinforcements, which can be a reward or punishment. Reinforcements increase the likelihood of a behavior occurring; punishments decrease the likelihood of a behavior occurring. Skinner introduced the ideas that reinforcements and punishments could be both positive and negative. Importantly, positive and negative do not imply pleasant or unpleasant, but addition or removal of a stimulus. When a stimulus is given to increase a behavior, it is a positive reinforcement; however, if something is removed to increase a behavior, it is a negative reinforcement. The same is true for punishments, except the goal is to decrease a behavior.

297. Answer should include the following key points: Skinner found that behaviors were stronger when reinforcements were delivered in continuous short and achievable schedules. The schedule could be by ratio or interval, fixed or variable, but if the schedule was too hard or too long the behaviors would weaken. Ratio schedules dispense reinforcement after so many behavior occurrences, while interval schedules are set amounts of time. A fixed schedule implies a set number of occurrences, or a set amount of time, must precede dispensing of the reinforcement. Variable schedules have no set amount of time or number of occurrences and are unpredictable in dispensing reinforcement. Ratio schedules tend to produce higher rates of responding than intervals. Variable interval schedules are more reliable than fixed intervals in maintaining desired response behaviors.

298. Answer should include the following key points: In Skinner's experiments the pigeons performed some action and a response occurred. When the response was pleasurable, the animal would repeat the action; but if it was painful, the animal would not repeat the action. Skinner developed an apparatus box containing a lever that when pressed or pecked would release a food pellet or a seed. He also experimented with conditioned learning by adding visual and auditory stimuli paired with the pressing or pecking behaviors leading to the dispensing reinforcement (food).

299. Answer should include the following key points: Because the organism learns that persistence pays off and will persist in the behavior under the belief that sooner or later it will pay off. Skinner found that behaviors were stronger when reinforcements were delivered in continuous short and achievable schedules. The schedule could be by ratio or interval, fixed or variable, but if the schedule was too hard or too long, the behaviors would weaken.

300. Answer should include the following key points: Complex behaviors are modified by reinforcement schedules that shape behaviors based on successful approximations. Rewarding the behaviors that serve as steps to completing the desired behavior supports the learning process. When the goal is a complex behavior, rewarding approximate behaviors is essential to keeping organisms motivated in the learning process.

301. Answer should include the following key points: Positive reinforcement—addition of something to increase desired behaviors; negative reinforcement—removal of something to increase a desired behavior; positive punishment—addition of something to decrease an undesired behavior; negative punishment—removal of something to decrease an undesired behavior. The schedule for rewards could be a ratio after a certain number of days of exercising and eating healthy.

Social Behavior and Learning

302. (A) Bandura proposed that learning is a reciprocal process between the individual and the environment. Rotter believed that people form subjective expectations about the reinforcements that follow their behaviors.

303. (B)

304. (C)

305. (A)

306. (D)

307. (B)

308. (B)

309. Internal, external

310. external

311. internalized, emotional. The individual is consciously aware of the response, anticipates the outcome, and has expectations of the outcome on a future occurrence of the response. People learn new behaviors by observing and imitating, or modeling, the behavior of other people they consider admirable, powerful, nurturing, or similar.

312. consequences

313. self-efficacy, internal

314. it becomes part of the child's problem-solving schema

315. self-efficacy

316. Answer should include the following key points: Bandura agreed with the behaviorist perspective in that the environment cues an action or response by an individual, and that rewards or reinforcements were important in acquiring or modifying behaviors. However, unlike the extreme behaviorist perspective, he believed the response is not an automatic, instinctive drive, but is instead the result of internalized thoughts and emotional interactions. In other words, the individual is consciously aware of the response, anticipates the outcome, and has expectations of the outcome on a future occurrence of the response.

317. Answer should include the following key points: The social learning theory holds that people learn new behaviors by observing and imitating, or modeling, the behavior of other people they consider admirable, powerful, nurturing, or similar. It may be clear when a person is inexperienced such as a child or new employee learning new tasks; however, social learning extends beyond the observed task. The individual gains significant information about the consequences of behaviors. Positive outcomes increase the likelihood that the observer will repeat the behavior, whereas negative outcomes decrease the likelihood.

318. Answer should include the following key points: Social learning is related to perceptions, interpretations, self-understanding, social reflection, and self-efficacy. Bandura believed that an individual's beliefs and self-understanding directly influence that person. Researchers have explored the effect of observed violence on childhood behaviors and found that once the behavior has been modeled, it becomes part of the child's problem-solving schema. In his classic experiment, Bandura and colleagues used Bobo dolls to demonstrate this phenomenon. Children who witnessed a model perform aggressive acts on the Bobo doll exhibited imitated aggression as well as significantly more ways (than observed in the model) to be aggressive. On the other hand, not all children react aggressively after viewing violence in others or the media. Learning is dependent upon more than observing and imitating, to include the individual's cognitive efforts in processing observed outcomes. The individual gains significant information about the consequences of behaviors. Punishment, rejection, and other negative outcomes that follow another's behaviors decrease the likelihood of observers adopting those behaviors. In addition, children with greater self-efficacy for avoiding aggression, and who have been reinforced for doing so, are less likely to solve problems with aggression.

319. Answer should include the following key points: Self-efficacy is an individual's sense of self-esteem and competence for a given situation. Bandura believed that level of self-efficacy will determine how strongly external experiences will influence behaviors. Higher degrees of self-efficacy are consistently found to associate with greater levels of achievement success, whereas lower degrees are associated with hopelessness and poorer psychological health. Locus of control is one's sense about the source of control and is a mix of internal and external reinforcement. Rotter believed that people tend to have a dominant internal or external locus of control. Locus of control determines the degree of effect external experiences will have on behaviors. People with an internal locus of control believe they have a great deal of influence on outcomes, while those with an external locus of control believe outcomes are beyond their influence.

320. Answer should include the following key points: Self-efficacy is an individual's sense of self-esteem and competence for a given situation. Higher degrees of self-efficacy are consistently found to associate with greater levels of achievement success. For the older adult who may have a low self-efficacy for exercise activities, increasing knowledge, perceptions, ability, and competence will lead to greater self-efficacy. Increased knowledge comes from instructions for exercise, recommended frequency and intensity, injury prevention, and benefits. Perceptions can include addressing stereotypes, awareness of resources; same-age case stories, community involvement, and other resources that are specific to the person's situation will work to integrate value and belief with newfound knowledge. Practice and participation lead to greater abilities and competence levels. Interventions lacking in any one of these elements will not have the same effect on self-efficacy.

Chapter 5 Cognitive Theories and Perspectives

Information Processing Theory

321. (C)

322. (D)

323. (C)

324. (C)

325. (D)

326. (D)

327. (A)

328. Cognitive psychology

329. Metamemory

330. brain maturation, selective attention, and automatization

331. hippocampus

332. limited, rehearsed

333. Myelination

334. Metacognition

335. Answer should include the following key points: Miller's magic number seven research holds that humans can easily recall seven plus or minus two pieces of information depending on the type of information stored. A long list of information can best be stored as chunks of information.

336. Answer should include the following key points: Like computers, human minds receive sensory input comparable to data input, working memory processes information much like data analysis, both store and hold information, and recall of information in the mind is essentially the same as data output. Unlike computers, however, human cognition requires brain maturation, selective attention, and automatization before it can be efficient.

337. Answer should include the following key points: Sensory receptors receive external information and send it along neural axons within the central nervous system. These impulses travel to the brain and become sensory memory, most of which lasts for less than one second before it decays. In addition to receiving sensory stimuli and sending them to the working memory, the sensory system is involved in storing information into long-term memory, and therefore in the retrieval, working as a cue to assist in bringing the information to mind again. Working memory is still within the neural system; it is not stored information, and it can last between 10 and 15 seconds before starting to decay. Rehearsing this information, such as when we repeat new phone numbers, can delay the decay rate for a brief time—usually for only another 10 to 15 seconds. Working memory also has a limited capacity, and strategic manipulation and organization of information such as rehearsal, activation, pattern-matching, and response generation is necessary to move information into long-term memory.

338. Answer should include the following key points: The computer metaphor provided a popular working model for explaining how information is stored in memory, the processes of recalling stored information, and how new information could be integrated with previously stored information to form new knowledge. The information processing theory, as it became known, asserts that human thinking processes are like computer processes. Like computers, human minds receive sensory input comparable to data input, working memory processes information much like data analysis, both store and hold information, and recall of information in the mind is essentially the same as data output.

339. Answer should include the following key points: The hippocampal region of the brain is similar to a recipe card or directory board. It contains all the detailed information about the memory. The first time you recall the memory, you need to retrieve the details in order, but the more frequently you use the details, the less the hippocampus is needed to provide the details. The hippocampus is most essential for storing information. If it is damaged, new memories cannot be stored; however, old ones can still be retrieved.

340. Answer should include the following key points: Metacognition allows us to assess cognitive tasks and determine the best strategies for accomplishing them. When planning to make changes in behaviors, it is important to have a clear goal in mind with measurable steps leading to it. Metacognition skills include mapping out the steps to goal attainment, identifying resources needed to achieve the goal, and other aspects that support progress such as identifying barriers and rewards. Metacognition allows us to evaluate our efforts and make adjustments in our strategies as needed. While goals such as exercise more, eat healthy, and quit smoking are important goals with tangible steps, much of what is required to reach these goals is cognitive. Our thoughts, beliefs, and attitudes will always influence our efforts in attaining goals.

341. Answer should include the following key points: Myelin is a fatty coating on the axons that speeds signals between neurons. Extensive myelination results in faster communication pathways necessary for efficient information processing. Quicker information processing makes selective attention and quicker reaction times possible, and the process of storing information to memory becomes easier. Metamemory is the understanding of how memory works to be able to apply effective strategies for storing and retrieving information such as preparing for exams. These abilities also advance reasoning and logical thinking, which make metacognition possible. Metacognition is the ability to assess a cognitive task in order to determine the best way to accomplish it. The efficiency of metamemory and metacognition processes relies on the myelin sheath. If myelination breaks down, reaction times and accuracy of the information communicated along the neuron become vulnerable. Common causes of myelin breakdown are illness, malnutrition, and aging.

Stages of Cognitive Development

342. (C)

343. (A)

344. (C)

345. (B)

346. (A)

347. (D)

348. (C)

349. sensorimotor (six stages from birth to two years), preoperational (ages 2 to 6), concrete operational (ages 7 to 11), and formal operational (age 12 to adulthood)

350. sensorimotor cognitive development

351. theory of mind

352. centration

353. Transitive inference

354. formal operational

355. intuitive and analytical

356. Answer should include the following key points: An infant's first learning experiences take place through the processes of sucking, tasting, and biting. Initially reflexes provide sensation and lead to perception. Until babies can grasp and navigate objects to their mouth independently, everything put into their mouth is a source of food or comfort. As a result, among the first interpreted perceptions gained in life is that we feel better when we put something in our mouth. With improved motor abilities, the infant will soon begin assimilating new information into existing knowledge. Grasping and bringing an object to his or her mouth provides a new experience in the sounds, texture, and hardness or softness of the object. This experience as adapted is perceived as "I can put this in my mouth, but it will not provide me food or the comfort that comes from sucking." As a result, a new mental representation develops to accommodate this new idea.

357. Answer should include the following key points: Infant intelligence begins with sensation (sensory input), perception (analysis/meaning), and motor movement. New experiences become knowledge through two methods: assimilation, adding new schemas into existing knowledge, and accommodation, modifying existing schemas to form new ones. An infant's early learning occurs through sucking, tasting, and biting. Advancing motor skills leads to new abilities and opportunities and therefore new experiences. Piaget believed the infant's participation, emotional expression, and focused attention in sensorimotor activities are indicative of early signs of purposeful intention, or goal-directed behaviors. They acquire object permanence and learn to anticipate reactions, and through trial-and-error learning, they become able to predict outcomes using their existing knowledge. By age two, the child is capable of anticipating consequences that correspond with combining more than one mental representation.

358. Answer should include the following key points: Factors that support development of theory of mind include healthy brain development, especially maturing of the prefrontal cortex, frequent social interaction with other children, mothers who have conversations with the child, having siblings, particularly older siblings, in the home, and the child's vocabulary and use of language. Factors that slow down development of theory of mind include watching a lot of TV, children who are left alone, and malnutrition.

359. Answer should include the following key points: Children's knowledge is based on observable characteristics such as appearance, function, and previous experiences. Piaget's classic experiments demonstrate that by simply changing the shape or appearance of liquid, clay, or rows of items, young children fail to reason that the amount or quantity remains the same. The child believes that if it looks bigger, than there is more. Children's reasoning is limited by centration, or their attention focus on one aspect or idea at a time. Young children view the world from their own perspective and struggle to consider that something can be undone once it has changed. Therefore, change in appearance is a permanent change in the object.

360. Answer should include the following key points: Piaget proposed that children move through the periods of intellectual development based on the quantity of information they acquire and the quality of knowledge and understanding. In other words, they know more and can do more with what they know. Piaget believed that cognition is limited by brain maturity, especially within the prefrontal cortex. The information processing theory is organized on the processing functions and efficiency of the brain. In the concrete operational period, the child's experiences influence logical reasoning. In the information processing theory, memory ability and reaction times improve, allowing for more efficient use of new information and better access to existing stored information. In this way, the information processing theory is complementary to Piaget's concrete operational period. The more information is stored in the memory banks, the more mental representations the child has to process new information. Experiences, particularly academic experiences, further develop and strengthen abilities to engage in metacognition and metamemory. Advancing abilities make it possible for 10- to 12-year-old children to solve any problem provided they have a concrete set of rules.

361. Answer should include the following key points: Analytic thought is formal, logical, rational, hypothetical, and deductive. Intuitive thought starts with a prior belief or assumption and involves applying memories or feelings. Adolescents use intuitive thinking so frequently because it is fast and powerful. Additionally, increased hormonal production brings emotion to the forefront of adolescents' thought processes, and intuitive thought is more emotional than analytic thought.

362. Answer should include the following key points: Adolescents face new challenges related to egocentrism associated with identity development. Young adolescents think intensely about themselves and about what others think of them. Adolescents believe they are unique, special, and more socially significant than they actually are. The prefrontal cortex is still under development, and adolescents are more impulsive, shortsighted, and self-centered in decision making than the young adult. Because adolescence is an emotional time, cognitive tasks such as decision making and problem solving are influenced by fears, worry, negative sense of self, depression, and anxiety stemming from irrational beliefs. As the adolescent moves into young adulthood, planning, organizing self-control, judgment, and emotional regulation integrate information from multiple areas of the brain.

Sociocultural Learning

363. (A)

364. (B)

365. (D)

366. (C)

367. (D)

368. (A)

369. (D)

370. Lev Vygotsky

371. language

372. parents

373. zone of proximal development

374. scaffolding

375. active participants

376. problem-solving skills

377. apprentices in learning

378. Answer should include the following key points: Vygotsky and Piaget focused on child cognitive development. Both agreed that children are active learners in their environments. Vygotsky used Piaget's framework of children as eager and active learners limited by their maturity levels. The primary differences between Piaget's and Vygotsky's perspectives are that Piaget believed development needed to happen before learning, and Vygotsky believed development happened because of learning. However, he extended Piaget's work to include the benefits gained by experiences from interactions with other children and adults from their culture.

379. Answer should include the following key points: Learning progresses from tasks and skills outside of the child's potential to learn, to tasks he or she can do with assistance, and finally to tasks that can be done independently by the child. Vygotsky described tasks that cannot be performed independently but are within a child's potential as being in the child's zone of proximal development. Vygotsky considered children as apprentices in learning, and held that adults (parents, teachers, and mentors) are crucial in guiding children through their zone of proximal development.

Example: Each time Mike tries to ride his bike with no training wheels, his father gives him a little less help.

380. Answer should include the following key points: Vygotsky believed that informal and formal communication between the parent and child was key in bringing about learning. He suggested that social interactions in early childhood were extremely important in forming language, which he asserted is the vehicle for cognitive development. Vygotsky believed that complex cognitive tasks begin as basic social interactions and for the most part fall within the child's zone of proximal development. Vygotsky believes that children rely on guided participation and instruction from their mentors to accomplish the more complex tasks. Vygotsky also emphasized that culture determines what is important for the child to learn, and that children will learn the necessary skills for transitioning into adulthood within their cultures.

381. Answer should include the following key points: Vygotsky believed that parents and other caregivers are the child's first mentors and primary source of information. In all learning activities, parents and caregivers should create the learning opportunity and let the child participate in accomplishing that task. They provide assistance without taking over, ensure that the child has all the information and resources, and then encourage and motivate. For example, a child can be involved in planning and preparing the meal (the task) and can help choose from a list of foods (resources). Parents can teach the child about each of the food items (information), and talk about the benefits of eating healthy foods (motivation). This activity can be transitioned out of the home for grocery shopping and when eating in other settings. Parents can create reward systems and guide the child through problem solving as needed.

382. Answer should include the following key points: Vygotsky referred to the temporary support tailored to the child's learning needs and abilities as scaffolding. Parents and other mentors provide scaffolding as they teach, provide instructions, create opportunities to practice, encourage motivation, and assist until the child masters the task.

383. Answer should include the following key points: Vygotsky proposes that children learn within a social context and that what they learn in this context influences how they think as they mature. Vygotsky also emphasized that culture determines what is important for the child to learn, and that children will learn the necessary skills for transitioning into adulthood within their cultures. Knowledge is gained through social interactions, such as play and responsibilities, and tasks that support adult roles are encouraged play activities.

Kohlberg's Moral Reasoning

384. (B)

385. (C)

386. (A)

387. (B)

388. (A)

389. (A)

390. (B)

391. Lawrence Kohlberg

392. preconventional

393. fairness

394. they think they will not be caught

395. conventional

396. postconventional

397. perspective. One perspective is social justice, legal rules, and rights. Another perspective is universal fairness.

398. Answer should include the following key points: Kohlberg suggested that moral reasoning stems from cognitive development and progresses through three stages. The first stage, preconventional, is a time in which the moral value of an action is associated with the consequences. Punishment following a behavior determines that behavior as bad, whereas praise and other reinforcements determine the behavior as good.

399. Answer should include the following key points: In the second stage, the conventional stage, the morality of a behavior is weighed against social rules and cultural norms. They begin to consider needs of others over their black-and-white boundaries of right and wrong. In doing so, they exhibit increased prosocial behaviors of forgiveness and generosity. For example, children begin to recognize that others may have a disadvantage, and many will naturally offer extra help or make exceptions to the rule in such situations. By late adolescence, appreciation of rules deepens as teenagers recognize the importance of social order for the good of the group, not just the person.

400. Answer should include the following key points: Transitioning through the levels of moral reasoning as proposed by Kohlberg depends on experiences, including reinforcements and punishment, and also on cognitive maturation. Transition of adolescents into independent young adult roles involves an integration of shared beliefs of the parental environment and aspects of the new social environment. As they move into early adulthood, there is an expectation that everyone's benefit should be considered in the decision rather than that of just one individual. Teamwork and loyalty to the group are valued more than individual interests or goals.

401. Answer should include the following key points: Young adults achieve mature moral reasoning to varying degrees; however, for most the postconventional level of moral development is not acquired until later in adulthood, and many adults do not function at the higher levels. The last two stages may not differ in final solutions or decision, although the reasoning behind the decision represents a different agenda. Many adults are content with perspectives of justice, oriented around laws and individual rights (stage 5), while others take a global perspective in which universal principles of fairness are emphasized (stage 6). Most adults recognize that there is value in being flexible and open to change, and they are therefore motivated to compromise. In addition, many realize that more involvement with diverse cultures broadens individual perspective, and therefore promotes better adaptation into diverse social roles.

402. Answer should include the following key points: Kohlberg's preconventional level parallels Piaget's preoperational period. Children are egocentric and focused on one side of morality, being good, authority figures are right, and rules must be followed. At the conventional level moral reasoning parallels with Piaget's concrete operational period. Children are black and white in their thinking initially, but experiences help them to see that fairness and generosity are important and sometimes the rules have to include people's situation. The postconventional level of moral reasoning parallels the formal operational period in which adolescents are able to use concrete and hypothetical reasoning to determine a moral solution. Experiences, culture, and personality influence the level of morality for an adult. Kohlberg also acknowledges that brain maturation is important at all levels.

403. Answer should include the following key points: Reasoning about right and wrong is shaped by chronological age, culture, experience, and biological variables. Kohlberg's theory does not acknowledge or take into account cultural variations. Self-sacrifice for the sake of a family member is practiced around the world to greater and lesser extents. Additionally, Kohlberg's research was based on male gender, and it may not adequately reflect the significance of the female inclination toward nurture.

404. Answer should include the following key points: Adolescents ages 9 to 17 are within the conventional, or community-centered level of Kohlberg's model. Within this level of development, there is an emphasis on social rules and obeying laws. While many adolescents would not be intrinsically motivated to break the rules, they are vulnerable to social approval and have a need for peer acceptance. They are loyal to their friends. In Paget's cognitive model, adolescents age 9 to 11 are concrete in reasoning. Their ideas of right and wrong are narrow but dependent on the underlying belief or value. Helping, sharing, and belonging are important in peer groups. Children ages 12 to 17 are in Piaget's formal operational level, capable of reasoning in abstract terms. However, they too are shortsighted in terms of considering consequence. They are also more likely to be motivated by gratification in the present than worry about potential negative outcome or consequences. Helping, sharing, and belonging are still important. This population is more likely to share medications out of loyalty and inability to understand the danger or potential legal consequences.

Schaie: Intelligence and Cognition in Adulthood

405. (A)

406. (C)

407. (C)

408. (B)

409. (B)

410. (A)

411. (D)

412. Seattle Longitudinal Study

413. environmental pressures

414. acquisition, achieving

415. social norms

416. executive

417. legacy-leaving

418. health status and awareness of physiological decline

419. Answer should include the following key points: Throughout most of adolescence, teenagers are protected from the demands and pressures associated with adult responsibilities and decision making. Most adolescents are in a formal education system and experience growth in the quantity and quality of social opportunities. School, peers, and other social networks provide information that will later be adapted into strategies for practical life experiences. Adolescent brains are still under construction but are efficient in taking in and storing information. Unfortunately, much of this information will not be relevant to the youth as emerging adulthood approaches. However, the accumulation of new knowledge and skills during adolescence promotes adjusting to the cognitive pressures and demands of emerging adulthood. Schaie explained emerging adulthood as a time for achieving; a time when information is adapted to plan and problem solve to meet long-term goals for livelihood. Decision making continues to be focused on filling self-needs but also starts to include the need of others, or social responsibilities. Young adults are now accountable for consequences of their decisions but struggle because most of the important decisions they need to make about career, relationships, and self-care do not have concrete answers or clearly defined steps for achievement. The responsibility stage allows the adult to practice alternate approaches to achieving goals, including acknowledging others' perspectives and outcomes of previous social experiences. Concern about the effect an individual's decision may have on others in his or her life has a greater influence on decision making.

420. Answer should include the following key points: Executive reasoning is marked by ability to organize information in a structured manner, which allows a person to set realistic goals. In this way, goals are structured, and clear steps can be identified for reaching them. Goals move from self-serving to include others, such as family, work, and community. Decisions focus on fulfilling a commitment to each relationship.

421. Answer should include the following key points: Schaie believed the changes in adult thinking result from the changing demands and roles that adults face in their life. As adults gain skills and perceptions from experiences, intellectual development takes place.

422. Answer should include the following key points: Schaie developed his theory based on social norms found in middle-class Western cultures. He asserted that adolescence is the time when the brain begins to acquire knowledge and expand on thoughts that will prepare the adolescent for upcoming problem solving for transitioning into adult roles. This is a limitation because the theory may not hold up across cultures. Cultures vary in the timing and nature of expectations and responsibilities for adolescents.

Postformal Thought: Cognition and Moral Reasoning in Young Adulthood

423. (C)

424. (A)

425. (C)

426. (C)

427. (C)

428. (D)

429. (A)

430. postformal thought

431. intellectual development

432. relevancy

433. transition from dualism to relativism

434. emergence of reflective judgment

435. concrete events based on an individual's experiences

436. becoming more flexible in perspective, or flexibility in thinking

437. learned rules and strategies

438. Answer should include the following key points: The first four positions are dominated by dualistic thoughts, with the first being extremely right or wrong thinking. Position 1, strict dualism, implies a rigid adherence to authority figures, and Perry asserted that no one enters college at this level. The second position is prelegitimate multiplicity, characterized by having many ideas, answers to questions, and points of view. Individuals are aware that some of the information available to them is right and that they have to go through it to discover the truth. Position 3, early multiplicity, is characterized by the belief that more than one idea may be correct. While students acknowledge that there are multiple perspectives, they believe that only some of the perspectives are accurate or relevant. In position 4, late multiplicity, students become better at deciphering information based on relevancy and accepting that even experts have unique perspectives that often differ from one another. Rationalizing information, constructing and evaluating arguments, is the final transition before students acquire relativism.

439. Answer should include the following key points: Positions 5 through 9 are dominated by relativism, and adults begin to be open to opinions of others. They have stronger abilities to evaluate information for accuracy and have an increased preference for a worldview perspective. Relativism begins as contextual relativism, where acceptance of truth depends on where it comes from and how it affects the student. Even at this early stage of relativism, students can identify with chosen authority figures as colleagues in the same endeavors. At the position 6 level, commitment foreseen, young adults begin to identify with particular aspects of themselves. They have gained enough information on which to base long-term decisions such as making commitments to career, religion, political, and personal areas of their life. Adults changing, adapting, and accommodating new perspectives with their own characterize positions 7 to 9. Individuals move from an initial commitment, then transition to multiple commitments, and then transition to a state of resolve. Considering others' perspectives helps young adults begin to commit to their own personal beliefs. In addition, as commitment grows, adults are able to return to dualistic thinking in order to evaluate information that conflicts with personal beliefs. Being able to retreat from conflicting information will temporarily allow adults to delay making a decision about the accuracy of the information.

440. Answer should include the following key points: Dualistic thinkers are more narrow in their approach, deconstructing the problem into separate tasks. Relativists are more likely to approach the problem as whole and to rely on evidence-based information to support their thinking and problem solving. Relativistic thinkers are able to transition back to dualistic thinking long enough to rethink perspectives and temporarily delay making a decision.

441. Answer should include the following key points: Perry's and Kitchener's research found that young adults initially rely on absolute truths or concrete knowledge to make decisions. However, as they encounter problems that have no absolute or concrete answers for resolving them, young adults are forced to make decisions by coordinating information that is concrete as well as uncertain. Perry's study emphasized the role of college education in providing frameworks for learning, thereby advancing ability to seek out evidence and form a perspective about what is known. Kitchener's research is similar in that educational experience is correlated to level of reflective judgment. Both assert that young adults transition to relativistic thinking once they are able to accept that knowledge is contextual, develop a set of rules for coordinating different perspectives, and come to conclusions by drawing upon the most supportive evidence.

442. Answer should include the following key points: Relativist thinking can benefit a professional because people are diverse and relativistic thinking is contextual. Social norms, including beliefs about self, others, and appropriateness of behaviors for each vary from culture to culture. A relativistic perspective can adapt health philosophy to match the culture of the population of interest. A relativistic approach is person centered and will include a particular methodology that is most appropriate to a particular group.

443. Answer should include the following key points: Adults need to be able to engage in postformal thought processes in order to make decisions when there is not a clearly defined solution. Because postformal thought requires experiences and ability to accept and integrate perspectives different from one's own, age is not necessarily indicative of cognitive development. Interventions must set well-structured goals; however, strategies for achieving goals will vary from one individual to the next. Individuals who see their work in absolute terms will not be able to consider other perspectives.

Chapter 6 Social Theories and Perspectives

Social Cognition

444. **(C)** Social psychologists are concerned with how social situations influence individuals' thoughts and behaviors.

445. **(B)** Attitudes are the result of comparing our thoughts, feelings, and behaviors about all the aspects of the world around us.

446. **(B)** Attributions are the processes by which we attempt to explain the behavior of other people.

447. **(B)** Social cognition develops as we interpret, analyze, remember, and use information gained through social interactions.

448. **(D)** Social cognition is the cognitive process by which people understand and make sense of others and themselves.

449. **(C)** Schemas are mental representations or frameworks formed through experiences that help us organize social information.

450. **(A)** Stereotypes are inferences made based on group categorical information.

451. underestimate. When we group people by categories (ethnicity, religion, gender, age, etc.), we overestimate the differences and underestimate the similarities between members of different groups.

452. fundamental attribution error. People tend to attribute the behaviors of others to characteristics even when the behavior is a result of the situation.

453. bias. The influence of a recalled previous experience on present knowledge, beliefs, and feelings.

454. self-fulfilling prophecy. The self-fulfilling prophecy phenomenon is when an individual acts in ways that lead to an outcome, or seeks to find information that confirms a preexisting belief. In these ways, the individual brings about what he or she expected to see.

455. overestimate. People tend to categorize by creating groups based on similarities, which leads them to perceive the members within the group as the same.

456. subtyping. People tend to want to preserve their stereotypes, so when contradicting information arises, an exception to the rule is generated. This process is subtyping.

457. attributions. The process of making judgments by making inferences about the cause of a person's behavior.

458. Answer should include the following key points: People are more likely to side with the majority when they do not understand the information presented to them. Siding with the majority provides a sometimes false sense of accuracy based on the idea that a belief is better if a greater number of members subscribe to it. Social norms develop when the standard for what is appropriate remains consistent. The group with more people subscribed to a particular belief or behavior is likely to be stronger, more influential, or the group with the right answers. This heuristic, or a simple rule of thumb, helps ensure that we belong and will not be cast out of our social group, and it is a default strategy when people are faced with complex information. Even in a new situation or when the information is not well understood, siding with the majority heuristic can provide confidence about one's action or judgment.

459. Answer should include the following key points: Dispositional attributions are explanations about observable behaviors based on personal reasons. Dispositional attributions imply permanent aspects of a person, such as personality, temperament, or intelligence, and suggest that behaviors are typical and will happen again. Situational attributes are explanations for an observable behavior based on the context of the situation. Situation attributions imply a temporary influence such as environmental or personal history and suggest a behavior is not typical otherwise.

460. Answer should include the following key points: People tend to want to preserve their stereotypes, so when contradicting information arises, an exception to the rule is generated. This process is called subtyping, and Jessie is likely subtyping the new couple based on demographic variables as they are new to her area.

Social Identity Theory

461. (B)

462. (C)

463. (B)

464. (A)

465. personal, social

466. context

467. Intergroup

468. cultural norms

469. Answer should include the following key points: Personal identity is shaped from appearance, age, traits, talents, and so on. These are more or less observed in one's phenotype. Social identity consists of group-specific characteristics. Everyone has a social identity, one that is defined by the members within a social context.

470. Answer should include the following key points: As individuals, who we are depends on the situation, and our self-concept is based on self-complexity. We cannot experience each aspect of who we are in any given moment; therefore, we define ourselves within a context. An individual may be highly organized in one setting, such as in the office, but be disorganized at home.

471. Answer should include the following key points: When identities are organized complexly, there is more likelihood of conflict between aspects of the self. Perceived conflict creates more identity interference than actual complexity of identity. In other words, the more complexly the self is organized, and when these important self-constructs are distinct from each other, the better a person can handle changes in one of the identity constructs. For example, if there are three important identities, project manager, mother, and volleyball team player, a person will feel less stress to the overall sense of self should something negatively impact one of the constructs, such as physical injury and being benched for the season. When identities are intertwined and something negatively impacts one of the aspects, it is much harder to deal with the stress.

472. Answer should include the following key points: Intragroup comparisons within an individualistic culture would base self-identity on level of independence, and therefore the individual would largely define himself or herself by how independent of the group he or she is by comparison to other members within the same group such as family, friends, or community members. Greater independence, without isolation, brings higher regard for the self. In contrast, a collectivist culture that places higher value on interdependence would hold a higher regard for those who promote group equilibrium by not focusing on the individual but instead the larger group, such as family, friends, or the community.

Both cultures may make negative judgments about the degree of independence demonstrated by members outside of each group; however, each will incorporate behaviors that allow them to positively interact with the outside group. Therefore, members of each culture make intergroup comparisons to shape self-identity within the context of one's life.

Social Influence

473. **(C)** Social influence is the control of one person's behavior by another by meeting that person's need for pleasure, approval, or providing truth necessary to ensure that the person has accurate information or has made the correct decision.

474. **(A)** Observational learning is learning that takes place when one person observes another being rewarded or punished for a particular behavior.

475. **(B)** Rewards are pleasurable outcomes that result from one's behavior that generally increase motivation to continue the behavior.

476. (D) Normative influence is a phenomenon in which a person's behavior provides information to another individual about how to behave in a particular situation.

477. (A) Normative influence is information about behaviors that are appropriate for the group, such as saying please and thank you, opening and holding the door open, and exchanging gifts.

478. (C) Conformity is the tendency to do what others are doing simply because they are doing it, and obedience is the tendency to do what authorities tell us to do simply because they tell us to do it. Both behaviors are a form of normative influence that help us gain social acceptance. Going against either situation increases risk for isolation and rejection from the dominant social group.

479. (A) People need other people, and therefore social acceptance or approval is essential to survival. People will say or do something they do not believe in if going against the majority results in isolation from the group. In Asch's study, 75 percent of the participants conformed and gave an incorrect answer in order to gain social approval and remain within the group.

480. Social influence. Social influence is the ability of one person or a group of people to have control over others' thoughts, feelings, and behaviors. It is achieved by the influencer's ability to meet one or more of the basic human desires: pleasure, approval, or awareness of a truth and avoidance of false belief.

481. pleasure, approval, accuracy. People are motivated to experience pleasure and avoid pain, people are motivated to be accepted and avoid rejection, and people are motivated to believe the truth and avoid believing in false information.

482. pleasure. The power of pleasure motivates people toward enjoyable rewards or away from pain, anxiety, or negative consequences.

483. observational learning. Observational learning is learning that takes place when one person observes another being rewarded or punished for a particular behavior.

484. Social norms. Social norms are cultural practices and guidelines that govern social behavior. Often these standards are not formally enforced, but encouraged and reinforced through social approval or rewarded with an expected social benefit.

485. conformity, obedience. Conformity is the tendency to go along with or do what others are doing simply because they are doing it. Obedience is the tendency to do what people in authority positions tell us to do, simply because they tell us to do it.

486. obedience. Obedience is the tendency to do what people in authority positions tell us to do, simply because they tell us to do it.

487. Answer should include the following key points: People are susceptible to social influence because humans have three essential desires that can only be met through interactions with others. First people are motivated toward pleasure and to avoid pain and discomfort. Second, people need others' approval and therefore act in ways to be accepted. Finally, people want to know that what they believe in is the truth; they strive to know the correct or right information.

488. Answer should include the following key points: People want to be accepted by others in their environment, and want to act appropriately for the situation. There is a reciprocal relationship between the person and the environment. When there is no clear rule set for how to act in a given situation, people will follow the normative behaviors. It is customary in many cultures to form a line when waiting at an entrance. Those who do not follow the norm are perceived negatively, thought of as rude, and can be rejected by the group.

Cognitive Dissonance Theory

489. **(C)** Cognitive dissonance is an unpleasant state that arises when a person's behaviors are inconsistent with his or her attitudes and beliefs.

490. **(D)** Cognitive dissonance theory holds that people will change their attitudes to match their conflicting behaviors.

491. **(C)** Festinger proposed three types of dissonance situations that have received the most attention: postdecisional dissonance, effort justification, and insufficient justification. Social influence is the control of one person's behavior by another.

492. **(B)** Postdecisional dissonance results from having conflicting thoughts about two alternative decisions.

493. Leon Festinger. Festinger, an American psychologist in the 1950s, explored the distress people experience when accepting new information conflicts with existing beliefs. Festinger studied how the mind reconciles two conflicting beliefs by modifying existing attitudes.

494. altering beliefs

495. effort justification

496. stress

497. Answer should include the following key points: Mark can alleviate the dissonance by incorporating additional information into his beliefs. He can recognize that his behavior is a risk to his health and the smoking is harmful. It is likely Mark will feel the remorse when he smokes, and he will have to continue to adjust his beliefs to avoid the dissonance. Taking steps toward quitting smoking will provide him relief by bringing his behaviors in line with his new attitude.

498. Answer should include the following key points: According to Festinger, people work to reduce dissonance by altering beliefs, incorporating additional information, or downplaying the importance of the dissonant thought. Lisa believes that her friend's feelings are more important than telling her that she is happy Lisa broke up with her boyfriend, so she will change her attitude about the dishonesty in her remarks to spare her friend from hurt feelings.

499. Answer should include the following key points: Stacie is experiencing cognitive dissonance, the conflict that occurs when a person holds two contradictory attitudes or thoughts. Cognitive dissonance is stressful, and the discomfort motivates people toward reducing it either by altering beliefs, incorporating additional information, or downplaying the importance of the dissonant cognition.

500. Answer should include the following key points: Insufficient justification is the type of cognitive dissonance that explains that when people are paid a lot of money, they justify the lie because they are paid enough money to remove the dissonance. When people are paid a small amount, they are more likely to have a change in attitude because the small amount of money is not enough to remove the dissonance.

REFERENCES

Chapter 1

Schacter, D. L., Gilbert, D. T. & Wegner, D. M. (2011). *Introducing Psychology*. New York, NY: Worth Publishers.

Schultz, D. P. & Schultz, S. E. (2004). *A History of Modern Psychology* (8th ed.). Belmont, CA: Wadsworth/Thomson Learning Inc.

Chapter 2

Berger, K. S. (2014). *Invitation to the Life Span* (2nd ed.). New York, NY: Worth Publishers.

Broderick, P. C. & Blewitt, P. (2003). *The Life Span: Human Development for Helping Professionals*. Upper Saddle River, NJ: Pearson Education Inc.

Framingham, J. (2013). Minnesota Multiphasic Personality Inventory (MMPI). *Psych Central*. Retrieved on October 1, 2015, from http://psych-central.com/lib/minnesota-multiphasic-personality-inventory-mmpi/.

Keirsey.com (n.d.). The Keirsey Temperament Sorter (KTS-II). Retrieved from http://www.keirsey.com/aboutkts2.aspx.

The Myers & Briggs Foundation (2015). MBTI Basics. Retrieved from http://www.myersbriggs.org/my-mbti-personality-type/mbti-basics/.

National Human Genome Research Institute (2014). Retrieved from http://www.genome.gov/10001772.

Russell, C. C. (2011). Welcome to Parenting. Temperament. Retrieved from https://www.youtube.com/watch?v=gp3LmoAcfPA.

Chapter 3

Berger, K. S. (2014). *Invitation to the Life Span* (2nd ed.). New York, NY: Worth Publishers.

Broderick, P. C. (2003). *The Life Span: Human Development for Helping Professionals*. Upper Saddle River, NJ: Pearson Education Inc.

Schacter, D. L., Gilbert, D. T. & Wegner, D. M. (2011). *Introducing Psychology*. New York, NY: Worth Publishers.

Schultz, D. P. & Schultz, S. E. (2004). *A History of Modern Psychology* (8th ed.). Belmont, CA: Wadsworth/Thomson Learning Inc.

Chapter 4

Berger, K. S. (2014). *Invitation to the Life Span* (2nd ed.). New York, NY: Worth Publishers.

Broderick, P. C. (2003). *The Life Span: Human Development for Helping Professionals.* Upper Saddle River, NJ: Pearson Education Inc.

Schacter, D. L., Gilbert, D. T. & Wegner, D. M. (2011). *Introducing Psychology.* New York, NY: Worth Publishers.

Schultz, D. P. & Schultz, S. E. (2004). *A History of Modern Psychology* (8th ed.). Belmont, CA: Wadsworth/Thomson Learning Inc.

Chapter 5

Berger, K. S. (2014). *Invitation to the Life Span* (2nd ed.). New York, NY: Worth Publishers.

Broderick, P. C. (2003). *The Life Span: Human Development for Helping Professionals.* Upper Saddle River, NJ: Pearson Education Inc.

Daniel, K. L., Honein, M. A. & Moore, C. A. (2003). "Sharing Prescription Medication Among Teenage Girls: Potential Danger to Unplanned/Undiagnosed Pregnancies." *Pediatrics 111* (Supplement 1): 1167–1170.

Schacter, D. L., Gilbert, D. T. & Wegner, D. M. (2011). *Introducing Psychology.* New York, NY: Worth Publishers.

Schaie, K. W. & Willis, S. L. (2000). "A Stage Theory Model of Adult Cognitive Development Revisited." In B. Rubinstein, M. Moss & M. Kleban (eds.), *The Many Dimensions of Aging: Essays in Honor of M. Powell Lawton* (pp. 175–193). New York, NY: Springer.

Schultz, D. P. & Schultz, S. E. (2004). *A History of Modern Psychology* (8th ed.). Belmont, CA: Wadsworth/Thomson Learning Inc.

Chapter 6

Baron, R. A., Byrne, D. & Branscombe, N. R. (2006). *Social Psychology* (11th ed.). Boston, MA: Pearson Education Inc.

Schacter, D. L., Gilbert, D. T. & Wegner, D. M. (2011). *Introducing Psychology.* New York, NY: Worth Publishers.

Schultz, D. P. & Schultz, S. E. (2004). *A History of Modern Psychology* (8th ed.). Belmont, CA: Wadsworth/Thomson Learning Inc.